GENDER

A GRAPHIC GUIDE

MEG-JOHN BARKER
JULES SCHEELE

ICON

Published in the UK and the USA in 2019 by
Icon Books Ltd, Omnibus Business Centre,
39–41 North Road, London N7 9DP
email: info@iconbooks.com
www.iconbooks.com

Sold in the UK, Europe and Asia by
Faber & Faber Ltd, Bloomsbury House,
74–77 Great Russell Street,
London WC1B 3DA or their agents

Distributed in the UK, Europe and Asia by
Grantham Book Services
Trent Road, Grantham NG31 7XQ

Distributed in Australia and New Zealand by
Allen & Unwin Pty Ltd,
PO Box 8500, 83 Alexander Street,
Crows Nest, NSW 2065

Distributed in Canada by
Publishers Group Canada,
76 Stafford Street, Unit 300
Toronto, Ontario M6J 2S1

Distributed in India by
Penguin Books India,
7th Floor, Infinity Tower – C, DLF Cyber City,
Gurgaon 122002, Haryana

Distributed in South Africa by
Jonathan Ball, Office B4, The District,
41 Sir Lowry Road, Woodstock 7925

Distributed in the USA by
Publishers Group West,
1700 Fourth Street,
Berkeley, CA 94710

ISBN: 978-178578-452-1

Originating editor: Kiera Jamison

Printed and bound by Clays Ltd, Elcograf S.p.A.

GENDER: A FRAUGHT TOPIC

Every day we receive a barrage of confusing, complex – often contradictory – messages about gender. Gender is connected to everything in our lives. We can't get away from it even if we want to.

MULTIPLE MEANINGS

"Gender" means many different things at once:

Gender is both in the world around us and within us in our own experience. Gender is socially constructed: our culture develops and passes on strong messages about what it means to be each gender - and related roles and behaviours - through media, laws, education, and so on. At the same time we all have a lived experience of our gender which impacts how we experience our body, our feelings, our relationships, and pretty much everything in life. The way gender is socially constructed in the time and place that we live is part of what shapes our lived experience, but it's not the whole story, and different people relate to gender in different ways.

This means gender is both deeply political and personal, which can make it complex – and emotionally charged – to talk about.

MULTIPLE INTERSECTIONS

Gender can't be separated from other structures of power and our position within them. The way gender operates – and how we experience it – is intrinsically bound up with:

RACE, CLASS, SEXUALITY, DISABILITY, NATIONALITY, ETHNICITY, AGE, GENERATION, GEOGRAPHICAL LOCATION, FAITH, AND MORE.

* Hat tip to Kimberlé Crenshaw and all the other intersectional feminists and critical race theorists who have pointed this out over the years.

OUR GENDER JOURNEY

Gender warrior Kate Bornstein captures the complexity of gender when she says:

GENDER IS A BIG BALL OF WIBBLY-WOBBLY, GENDER-BLENDERY STUFF.*

If we're going to fully understand gender we're going to need to take a journey through time and space.

THE HISTORY OF GENDER

THE SCIENCE & PHILOSOPHY OF GENDER

MASCULINITIES

FEMININITIES

NON-BINARY GENDERS

TRANSGENDER & CISGENDER

THE FUTURE

THINKING ABOUT GENDER

* Kate is quoting Nat Titman here, who is, in turn, deliberately misquoting Doctor Who!

CHAPTER ONE: GENDER ACROSS SPACE & TIME

To understand gender, we need to know how it has operated through history, and around the globe.

People often assume that the way gender is understood and expressed in the time and place they currently occupy is the only right, normal, natural way of understanding and expressing it. History, archaeology, human geography, and anthropology show us that this is definitely not the case. Things have been - and could always be - different.

These studies also help us to understand how gender came to be socially constructed in the way it currently is, and why this often feels so entrenched and immovable - because it carries that weight of history.

ACKNOWLEDGING THE PAST

Professor of History Merry E. Wiesner-Hanks says we need to hold on to two key facts from the history of gender:

THERE IS MASSIVE GENDER DIVERSITY WITHIN AND BETWEEN GROUPS: FOR ANYTHING YOU MIGHT WANT TO CLAIM ABOUT GENDER THERE'LL ALWAYS BE A COUNTER EXAMPLE FROM SOMEWHERE IN HISTORY AND/OR ACROSS THE WORLD TODAY.

AND MOST OF THE WORLD FOR MOST OF TIME HAS BEEN PATRIARCHAL WITH MEN HOLDING MUCH OF THE POWER, AND WOMEN AND OTHER GENDERS SUBORDINATED.

So we have to be cautious about any claims about the natural, normal, or "right" ways of doing gender, at the same time as acknowledging the massive impact that patriarchal history has on all of us.

PATRIARCHY: A POTTED HISTORY

Gatherer-hunters: Archaeologists used to assume that in prehistoric societies men hunted and made tools while women raised children and did the less vital work of gathering. We now know that gatherer-hunters depended much more on foraged than hunted food, which is why archaeologists inverted the phrase "hunter-gatherer". We also know that women did hunt in some gatherer-hunter societies. Women may well have developed some of the earliest tools as well.

TOOLS

The agricultural revolution: The first agricultural revolution between 10,000 and 2,000 BCE increased the gap between men and women in the social hierarchy. Plowing and caring for animals became almost universally a men's task, valued over what became seen as women's tasks like spinning, weaving, and child-raising.

Land was needed for farming, and men became the ones who inherited this land in most places. Trading took men out into public life while women were increasingly kept in the private world of home and family.

Hereditary aristocracies: The states that developed across the ancient world after 3,000 BCE heightened gender distinctions. Rulers depended on taxes and slave labour, which meant they controlled the population more strictly.

Cultural norms and laws enhanced unequal gender relations and policed women's sexuality, often insisting they stay virgins until marriage and strictly punishing them for adultery.

In many cultures and religions, men became seen as the original humans – created by a male god in his image. Women were an afterthought and often held responsible for everything that went wrong with the world.

THE HISTORY OF GENDER IS INTERWOVEN WITH THE HISTORY OF CAPITALISM

Gender divisions increased at the same time that class divisions emerged. Elite landowners presented themselves as naturally superior to justify maintaining sharp distinctions between themselves and everybody else.

With the shift to **trade-based capitalism** in the 16th and 17th centuries, trade guilds (and later unions) began to define labour as men's work. Activities such as brewing or weaving, which had been regarded as women's work, became more highly valued when associated with men.

The current Western understanding of gender is closely linked to 19th-century **industrial capitalism**, which required women to work unpaid in the home, caring for the workforce and producing its next generation. When women did work outside the home, it relied on them being paid less than men. Work continued to be valued more highly when associated with men, particularly work associated with advanced technology, which was portrayed as too complicated for women.

Our concepts of gender and class are intrinsically connected because of the way that capitalism attributed a greater financial value to some labour (male, upper/middle-class) than to others (female, working-class).

THE HISTORY OF GENDER IS INTERWOVEN WITH THE HISTORY OF COLONIALISM

Europeans from the 16th century onwards imposed their understandings of gender and family life on the people they colonized – as well as often wiping out indigenous groups, and their ways of doing gender.

As with capitalism, colonialism relies on seeing some bodies and lives as less valuable than others in order to justify colonizing – and often enslaving – others. Like women and children, colonized people were often regarded as property belonging to white men.

TAKE UP THE WHITE MAN'S BURDEN ...
ON FLUTTERED FOLK AND WILD –
YOUR NEW-CAUGHT SULLEN PEOPLES,
HALF DEVIL AND HALF CHILD.

RUDYARD KIPLING

Slaves were seen as so inferior or inhuman that gendered **norms** did not apply to them. Slave and peasant women often did heavy labour and work in public rather than being secluded in the home, for example. These assumptions can still be seen in the modern-day treatment of black and working-class women, as we'll explore in Chapter 4.

CLASSIFYING THE "OTHER"

From the late 19th century, the categorizing of people into "normal" or "abnormal" became a major scientific project intrinsically linked to **imperialism** (extending a country's power and influence through colonization). The project was justified on the basis of classifying peoples into naturally "superior" and "inferior" races. Like women, people with same-sex attraction, people of colour, and people of "lower classes" were often deemed more childlike, or morally and intellectually inferior, on the basis of things like head/brain size and shape.

This was also an **ableist** project: the underlying assumption was that some bodies and brains are inherently more normal, "healthy" or "ordered" than others. Everyone was classified in comparison to a white, middle-class, heterosexual, non-disabled male, who became the norm.

We can see the legacy of how gender was bound up with race, class, and disability in this project in the way certain bodies are still regarded as too masculine/feminine, or not masculine/feminine enough.

HETERONORMATIVITY

During this othering project, gender, sexuality, and relationships became inextricably linked: a "normal" gender requires a "normal" sexuality to express it, and a "normal" relationship to express that sexuality.

Under capitalism the relationship norm became a monogamous marriage between people of two genders leading to a nuclear family (father, mother, and 2.4 children cohabiting). Men and women were seen as increasingly opposite and complementary in order to justify women's unpaid labour in the home on the basis of their supposed naturally caring and passive character.

Consumer capitalism built on these ideas, creating fears that we are individually lacking or abnormal – not masculine, feminine, sexy, or loveable enough – so as to drive the desire for products to fix ourselves.

We can see the legacy of this fusion of gender, sexuality, and relationships in the stereotype of gay men as feminine and gay women as masculine, as well as in the double standard where men are viewed positively for being sexual, and women negatively.

BEYOND PATRIARCHY

Because of the way patriarchy has intersected with other forms of oppression, we can't ever understand it in isolation.

History has also been marked by the subjugation of children by adults, and animals by humans. Relatedly, of course, women are often regarded as childlike or animal-like.

While most of the world for most of time has been patriarchal, patriarchy has operated in diverse ways throughout history depending on how it intersected with other oppressions. This has led to diverse understandings and experiences of gender, especially as different cultures have come into contact with each other.

Although there have very rarely, if ever, been fully matriarchal societies, there have been **matrifocal** societies with women as heads of household. In some places wealthy women have wielded power, but everyday women have almost always been punished for having any power.

I FOUND CULTURES WHERE MEN AND WOMEN WERE PEACEFUL, WHERE BOTH WERE WARLIKE, AND WHERE WESTERN GENDER STEREOTYPES WERE OPPOSITE, WITH WOMEN WORKING AND MEN BEAUTIFYING THEMSELVES, FOR EXAMPLE.

MARGARET MEAD

NEWS TODAY
TOO SKINNY!

Follow
You don't know what you're talking about @womanwhospeaksout, you filthy old slut
Reply Retweet Favorite ••• More

GENDER DIVERSITY THROUGH TIME

The roles, expressions, and behaviours that are regarded as masculine or feminine have varied over time and between places. For example, in early Judaic societies, women were active in the public realm of work and trade so that men could renunciate worldly things for religious study.

IN MEDIEVAL AND RENAISSANCE TIMES, WOMEN WEREN'T ALLOWED TO PLAY FEMALE ROLES ON STAGE, SO WE BOYS PLAYED THESE PARTS.

MANY CULTURES HAVE STORIES OF THOSE WHO DISGUISED THEMSELVES AS MEN TO FIGHT IN WARS.

IN 18TH- AND 19TH-CENTURY ENGLAND, MEN MET FOR SEX AND SOCIALIZING IN MOLLY HOUSES. SOME OF US TOOK ON FEMALE ROLES AND APPEARANCE, AND FORGED A KIND OF FAMILY ENVIRONMENT.

In addition to norms shifting, there are many such well-known examples of groups going against the grain of gender.

We'll look at more historical examples challenging the man/woman binary on p.116.

GENDER DIVERSITY ACROSS SPACE

The West is largely set on having two gender categories: man and woman. However, many cultures around the world have more than two gender categories.

I'M HIJRA, WHICH MEANS I DON'T IDENTIFY WITH BEING A MAN OR WITH MASCULINITY. I LIVE IN A COMMUNE IN INDIA WITH OTHER HIJRA. WE WORSHIP BAHUCHARA MATA, A HINDU "MOTHER GODDESS" DEITY. WE WERE SEEN AS SACRED IN THE PAST, BUT FOLLOWING BRITISH COLONIZATION WE'RE HIGHLY STIGMATIZED.

IN THAILAND WE HAVE MANY DIFFERENT GENDER CATEGORIES: KATHOEY, DEE, ADAM, SAMYAAN, CHERRY ... TOMS LIKE ME ARE MASCULINE AND ATTRACTED TO WOMEN, BUT WE DON'T TREAT WOMEN THE WAY MANY MEN DO.

MACHI LIKE ME ARE PART OF THE MAPUCHE INDIGENOUS GROUP IN CHILE AND ARGENTINA. WE'RE SHAMANS WHO MOVE BETWEEN MASCULINITY AND FEMININITY OR COMBINE THE TWO.

COLONIZING AND DECOLONIZING GENDER

In 1990 many Native American and First Nations people agreed on an intertribal term "Two Spirit" to denote people who take on roles and costumes associated with men and women. Different tribes and nations also have different ways of understanding gender though.

Here again we see the link between gender, sexuality, race, and colonialism. White settlers endeavoured to eradicate this group because they did not fit into a binary classification of male or female.

READING GENDER ACROSS SPACE AND TIME

We need to be very careful, when looking across space and time, not to read our current gender situation onto other times and places.

It's tempting, for example, to search for matriarchies in the hope that something other than patriarchy might be possible in our own societies, or to idealize other times and places. The various imaginings of the Amazons in Wonder Woman are an example of this. It can also be tempting to search for reflections of current Western LGB or trans experiences in order to legitimate rights claims on the basis that these groups have always existed around the world.

Diverse experiences emerge within specific cultural contexts and so need to be understood contextually to avoid our being appropriative or exploitative.

Over the next pages we'll turn to two examples to illustrate how looking at an aspect of gender across space and time can help us to think more critically and contextually.

SEXUAL WOMEN

Historian Eleanor Janega compares gender norms in medieval times to pop culture today, demonstrating:

• How entrenched patriarchal systems are; and
• How social understandings of gender have varied greatly across time.

MEN ARE **RATIONAL** AND **PIOUS** BUT NEED **SEX** AS AN OUTLET FOR THEIR **VIOLENT** natures

WOMEN ARE *excessively* **SEXUAL** BY NATURE. IT'S UP TO **MEN** TO MAKE SURE THEY HAVE SEX IN THE **RIGHT WAY** ~ IN *marriage*, FOR **PROCREATION** ~ BUT NOT ON A **SUNDAY**, OR DURING **LENT**, OR WHILE *menstruating...*

For example, Janega notes that the double standard of sexuality has pretty much always meant that sexually desirous or available women have been treated with suspicion, whereas men have been assumed to have "logical" sexual desires.

STUD, CAD, *player*

NYMPH, TRAMP, TART, SLUT, **HO**, SLAG, *HUSSY*, HARLOT, *loose...*

The West has seen a shift over recent decades, from an assumption that women's sexuality is unbridled and must be controlled so as to provide sex the "right" way to men, to an expectation that they will be sexually desiring and "up for it". We still draw a sharp line between "appropriate" levels of enthusiasm and women wanting "too much" sex, but the latter is now treated as an outlier rather than the default.

> THERE ARE 10 TIMES AS MANY WORDS FOR SEXUALLY PROMISCUOUS WOMEN AS FOR MEN, AND MOST HAVE MUCH MORE NEGATIVE CONNOTATIONS.

21

Janega draws a comparison between norms in modern hip hop culture and norms in medieval Europe. She notes that it is *good* in hip hop for a woman to be sexually available to the guy who's into her. It's *bad* for her to be available to a guy who isn't into her, to have sex with "too many" people, or to be seen as wanting attention.

In medieval Europe this good/bad binary was flipped. The Church actually supported sex workers, who provided an outlet for men's supposedly uncontrollable urges, and gave supposedly hyper-sexual women a way to channel their sexual excess for good. But to be a sexually desirous woman outside of this context was unacceptable.

THAT'LL BE THREE DENARI, GOOD CHRISTIAN.

In both times and places, men valued women who were sexually available in a way that *they* deemed appropriate and unlikely to cause them problems. However, these examples show that women's sexuality *can* be seen in radically different ways.

22

PUBLIC TOILETS

Sociologist Francis Ray White suggests that exploring the rules, meanings, and very existence of public toilets can tell us a lot about how gender is understood, and how it intersects with class, race, disability, and sexuality.

PEOPLE NOW EXPECT PUBLIC TOILETS TO BE GENDER SEGREGATED, BUT THIS HASN'T ALWAYS BEEN THE CASE.

PRIOR TO THE 1820s PUBLIC LATRINES WERE FREE FOR ALL. AS CITIES GREW, PUBLIC TOILETS WERE CONSTRUCTED — FOR MEN — RESTRICTING WOMEN'S ACCESS TO PUBLIC SPACES.

WHEN WOMEN'S TOILETS APPEARED IN THE 1860s, PEOPLE OBJECTED THAT WORKING-CLASS WOMEN MIGHT TURN THEM INTO BROTHELS, AND MAKE THEM UNSAFE SPACES FOR MIDDLE-CLASS WOMEN.

PUBLIC TOILETS

Men only

THE VERY EXISTENCE OF GENDER-SEGREGATED PUBLIC TOILETS — WHEN TOILETS IN HOMES ARE NOT SEGREGATED — TELLS US ABOUT HETERONORMATIVE ASSUMPTIONS. THE PRESENCE OF "THE OPPOSITE SEX" IS SEEN AS DANGEROUS IN PUBLIC BUT NOT PRIVATE (WHERE MOST VIOLENCE AGAINST WOMEN ACTUALLY HAPPENS).

HISTORICALLY, IN PLACES LIKE SOUTH AFRICA AND THE USA, PUBLIC TOILETS WERE DIVIDED ALONG RACIAL LINES. CHANGES TO THIS SYSTEM WERE HOTLY PROTESTED.

THE CURRENT BACKLASH AGAINST THE INCLUSION OF GENDER NEUTRAL PUBLIC TOILETS, AND THE MORAL PANIC ABOUT WHICH TOILETS TRANS PEOPLE USE, TELLS US A LOT ABOUT HOW GENDER IS SEEN (MORE IN CHAPTER 6).

ACCESSIBLE TOILETS ARE RARELY GENDERED, REMINDING US HOW DISABLED PEOPLE ARE OFTEN VIEWED AS NON-SEXUAL, AND LESS "MAN" OR "WOMAN" THAN NON-DISABLED PEOPLE.

TOILETS ARE SITES WHERE THE THREAT OF POLLUTION IS HIGH. THEY THREATEN THE PURITY BARRIER BETWEEN THE INSIDE AND OUTSIDE OF THE BODY, SO THERE IS A POLICING OF BODIES WHICH THREATEN TO POLLUTE GENDER, SUCH AS WORKING-CLASS, BLACK, TRANS, AND DISABLED BODIES.

LEARNING FROM HISTORY AND GEOGRAPHY

So what have we learnt from our journey across space and time?

> PATRIARCHY IS EVERYWHERE, ALL OF THE TIME.

> PATRIARCHY HAS ALWAYS INTERSECTED WITH OTHER OPPRESSIVE FORCES: CAPITALISM, COLONIALISM, WHITE SUPREMACY ... SO WE CAN NEVER TEASE GENDER APART FROM OTHER CATEGORIES LIKE CLASS, RACE, SEXUALITY, OR DISABILITY.

> THE WEIGHT OF THIS HISTORY HANGS HEAVY ON US ALL.

> WHATEVER WE MIGHT WANT TO SAY ABOUT HOW GENDER WORKS, THERE HAS ALWAYS BEEN SOMEBODY SOMEWHERE WHO'S DONE IT DIFFERENTLY.

It's important to remember that this book itself is situated in space and time, and that we haven't got to the "right" understanding of gender now. Our understandings will always be constructed and contextual, and people in the future will see what we haven't seen - or can't see - now.

CHAPTER 2: HOW SEX/GENDER WORKS

We've now seen how gender norms and ideals are socially constructed. They develop in society and are built up through cultural practices. But how do we come to have an inner sense of our own gender? And how come it sometimes meshes with these wider social constructs and sometimes it really doesn't?

ANNE FAUSTO-STERLING

DAPHNA JOEL

CORDELIA FINE

SARI VAN ANDERS

SIMONE DE BEAUVOIR

GINA RIPPON

KIMBERLÉ CRENSHAW

JUDITH BUTLER

bell hooks

IRIS MARION YOUNG

TRAY YEADON-LEE

These are the kinds of issues that gender scholars, from biologists to philosophers, have grappled with for the past few decades. In this Chapter, we'll bring their ideas together to present our best current understanding of how gender works.

SEX AND GENDER

"Sex" is generally seen as referring to whether a person is **biologically** male or female, and "gender" to whether they **identify socially** as a man or a woman.

Usually these things are seen as mapping onto each other: biologically male people grow up to identify as men, behaving in ways our society regards as masculine; biologically female people grow up to identify as women, behaving in ways our society regards as feminine.

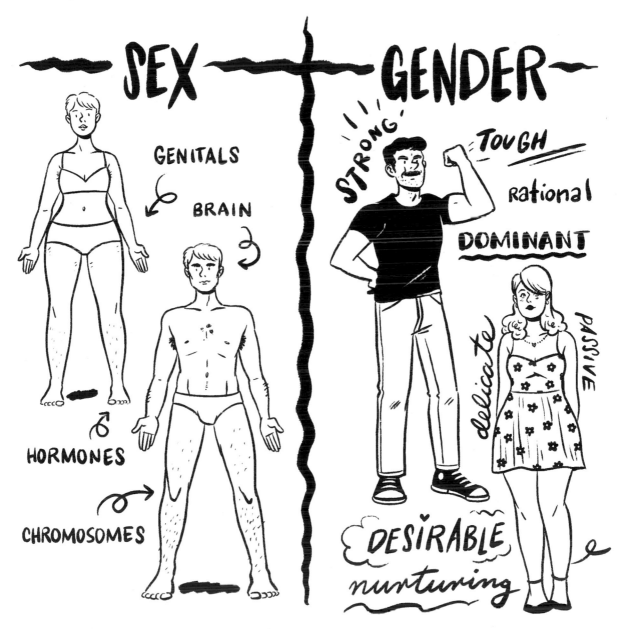

Let's think some more about what we mean by these words sex and gender: whether they can be separated out, and whether they do actually map onto each other in these ways.

SEX MEANS MANY THINGS

The idea of biological sex comprises features that are generally assumed to occur together: females having one combination of features, and males another.

Genitals: a penis and testes, or a clitoris and vagina. This is how medics usually determine whether "it's a boy" or "it's a girl". A clitoris is generally defined as a protuberance less than 9mm in length, and a penis longer than 25mm.

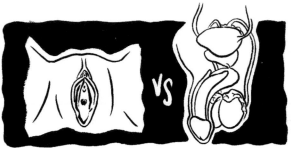

Genetics: XX (female) or XY (male) sex chromosomes.

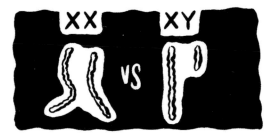

Hormones: our circulating levels of androgens like testosterone, oestrogens, and so on.

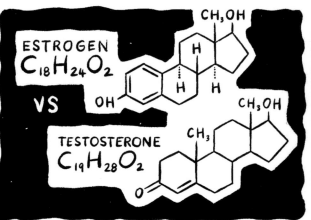

$$ESTROGEN \quad C_{18}H_{24}O_2$$

$$TESTOSTERONE \quad C_{19}H_{28}O_2$$

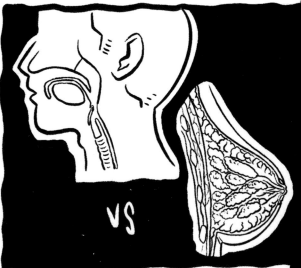

Secondary sex characteristics: bodily aspects seen as visibly distinguishing women and men – often developed during puberty – including height, weight distribution, having breasts or not, depth of voice, and hairiness.

Brain structure and activity: whether our brains have a more "male" or "female" structure or way of working; for example, the idea that women use more diverse parts of the brain, which may explain why they're supposedly better at multitasking.

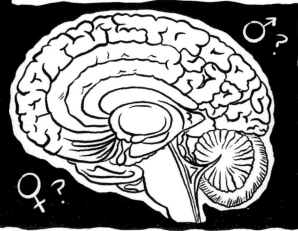

SEX VARIATION

We now know that all of these aspects of our biology vary and don't always map onto each other.

Neuroscientists like Daphna Joel have found that the vast majority of us combine aspects of what were previously thought of as "male" and "female" brains, and that many men fit a more "female" pattern and vice versa. Relatedly, psychologists like Eleanor Maccoby and Carol Jacklin found that there are very few cognitive abilities – like perception, learning, reasoning, and problem-solving – that show significant differences between men and women, and where these do exist they are small.

Similarly, when it comes to bodily characteristics like hairiness, height, and breast tissue, some women will appear more "masculine" than some men and vice versa, and there's a lot of cultural variation.

Likewise, hormone levels are not clearly tied to sex. Some women have higher levels of circulating testosterone than some men, for example, and some male athletes actually have testosterone levels well below the average for men.

INTERSEX

Intersex people raise awareness of the fact that there's actually much variation in: sex chromosomes; circulating hormones and how they're taken up in the body; and genital size and shape.

Intersex people are those whose anatomy or physiology differs from the conventional expectations of a male or female person. Some intersex people have sex chromosome combinations other than XX and XY (e.g. X, XXY, XYY); some have different chromosomal make-up in different parts of the body; some have bodies that respond in diverse ways to hormones. While it can be hard to gather data, biologist Anne Fausto-Sterling estimates that 1.7% of people are intersex.

Intersex people highlight the problems with defining sex by genital size. When it is considered "ambiguous", medics often carry out surgery to make the genitals conform to a notion of what male/female bodies should look like. This is frequently done based on whether the clitoris/penis is deemed "adequate for later sexual performance", showing how entwined gender is with a certain kind of heterosexual sex in Western culture. This practice is now illegal in some countries and considered a human rights abuse by many.

IT'S A GIRL! (under 3/8")

"UNACCEPTABLE" (surgery!)

IT'S A BOY! (over 1")

Phall-O-Meter®

WE FIGHT AGAINST ANY MEDICALLY UNNECESSARY, POTENTIALLY DAMAGING SURGERIES UNTIL A PERSON IS CAPABLE OF CONSIDERING THEIR OPTIONS AND MAKING A CHOICE.

intersex is beautiful

Let Intersex Children CHOOSE!

EDUCATE DON'T OPERATE

STOP HARMING INTERSEX CHILDREN

AN RIGHTS OLATIONS

GENDER MEANS MANY THINGS

We've seen that "sex" is used to mean many different things which may – or may not – map onto each other. "Gender" is also used in many different ways. Here are some of the common meanings.

Social norms: How wider culture assumes that women, men, or other genders feel and behave.

Roles: The kinds of work, family, and other roles typically taken on by people of different genders.

Identity: How a person themselves identifies in relation to gender, for example as a girl, a non-binary person, or a lad.

EXCUSE ME, MISS

Experience: How a person experiences themselves in relation to gender, for example whether they feel masculine or androgynous, or whether they're comfortable or uncomfortable with how others perceive their gender.

Expression: How a person expresses their gender, for example through clothing and body language.

MULTIPLICITY OF GENDER

From what we've covered so far, we can see that how a person's sex and gender are classified will vary depending on which feature of sex or gender we're talking about.

We've also seen that people's sex characteristics may align with expectations, or not, and the same is true of their gender characteristics.

For example, a person may identify as a woman and experience that as a good fit, express herself in ways that are seen as stereotypically feminine, and adopt roles generally associated with women in her culture. However, another person might vary on one or more of these aspects. She might identify as a woman but often feel uncomfortable with the assumptions other people make about what that means, and she may not enjoy stereotypically feminine roles or appearance.

SEX/GENDER

In addition to their individual multiplicity, sex and gender are much more intertwined than has often been assumed. It's not possible to clearly separate the way our bodies and brains operate – in terms of circulating hormones, neural activity, or muscle mass, for example – from our experiences of gender and the messages we receive about it in the world around us.

SEX/GENDER IS BIOPSYCHOSOCIAL

Sex/gender is always biopsychosocial. Our body and brain influence – and are influenced by – our personal experience, our social sphere, and culture. They continue to influence one another over the course of our lives. We could never disentangle these aspects of any one person's gender.

Let's look at some examples of how each of these things influences the others, before we explore some of these dynamics in greater depth.

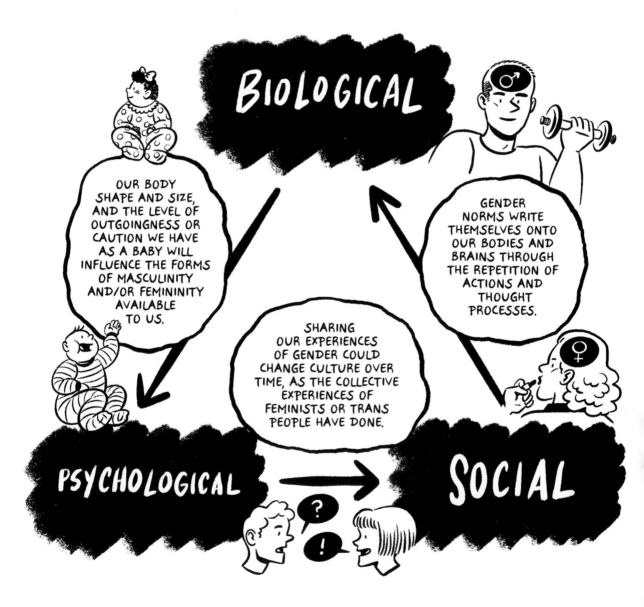

BIOLOGICAL

OUR BODY SHAPE AND SIZE, AND THE LEVEL OF OUTGOINGNESS OR CAUTION WE HAVE AS A BABY WILL INFLUENCE THE FORMS OF MASCULINITY AND/OR FEMININITY AVAILABLE TO US.

GENDER NORMS WRITE THEMSELVES ONTO OUR BODIES AND BRAINS THROUGH THE REPETITION OF ACTIONS AND THOUGHT PROCESSES.

SHARING OUR EXPERIENCES OF GENDER COULD CHANGE CULTURE OVER TIME, AS THE COLLECTIVE EXPERIENCES OF FEMINISTS OR TRANS PEOPLE HAVE DONE.

PSYCHOLOGICAL

SOCIAL

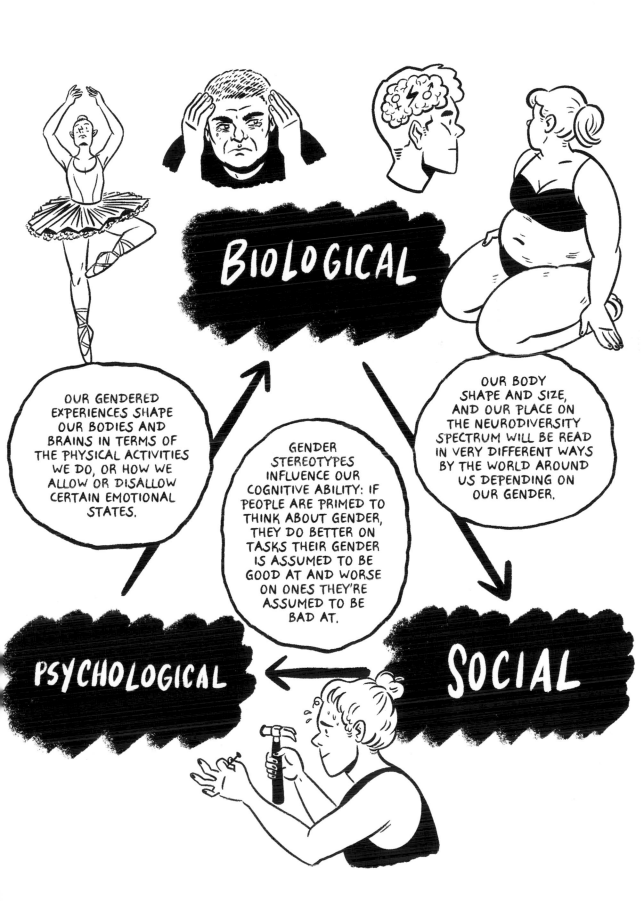

BIOLOGICAL

OUR GENDERED EXPERIENCES SHAPE OUR BODIES AND BRAINS IN TERMS OF THE PHYSICAL ACTIVITIES WE DO, OR HOW WE ALLOW OR DISALLOW CERTAIN EMOTIONAL STATES.

GENDER STEREOTYPES INFLUENCE OUR COGNITIVE ABILITY: IF PEOPLE ARE PRIMED TO THINK ABOUT GENDER, THEY DO BETTER ON TASKS THEIR GENDER IS ASSUMED TO BE GOOD AT AND WORSE ON ONES THEY'RE ASSUMED TO BE BAD AT.

OUR BODY SHAPE AND SIZE, AND OUR PLACE ON THE NEURODIVERSITY SPECTRUM WILL BE READ IN VERY DIFFERENT WAYS BY THE WORLD AROUND US DEPENDING ON OUR GENDER.

PSYCHOLOGICAL

SOCIAL

HOW SOCIAL NORMS SHAPE OUR SEX/GENDER

In the much repeated 1970s Baby X study, researchers gave adults a baby dressed in either pink or blue to play with, and found that the adults treated the babies completely differently based on the colour they were wearing and thus the perceived sex.

In her books, neuroscientist Cordelia Fine discusses how people's behaviours, attitudes, and performance on tasks become more gender stereotyped when they're primed to be aware of gender. Living in a highly gendered world from our earliest years – where people are divided into boys and girls and given different clothes, toys, and treatment accordingly – primes us in this way constantly. These habits shape neural connections over time.

Campaigns like "Let Toys Be Toys" ask toy and publishing industries to stop promoting some toys and books as only suitable for girls or only for boys, arguing that this limits children's interests and development.

OUR GENDERED EXPERIENCE SHAPES OUR BRAINS

Neuroplasticity refers to the way in which our brain structures, chemistry, and activity are influenced by the world we live in and what we do over the course of our lifetime.

Before the 1970s, neuroscientists generally believed that the brain's structure and function was fixed – or **hardwired** – once people reached adulthood. In recent decades, however, there has been increasing awareness of just how changeable – or **plastic** – brains are. As neuroscientist Gina Rippon points out, our brains change all the time as we learn. You can change someone's brain in hours by teaching them to juggle, play Tetris, or learn to be a taxi driver.

What's true for learning skills or information also holds for learning gender roles: being encouraged into different interests or school subjects and playing with differently gendered toys as a child, or participating in different jobs and leisure activities as an adult.

OUR GENDERED EXPERIENCE SHAPES OUR BODIES

The gendered ways in which we live our lives impact our bodies. Engaging in certain sports will increase our muscle mass or change our weight distribution; having a baby will alter our physical body and hormonal levels profoundly. Likewise, we'll see changes if doing manual labour or a caring job.

Testosterone is often found in higher levels in men than women, and is seen as the reason for them being more ambitious, competitive, and aggressive. However, studies by scientists like Sari van Anders have found testosterone levels increase when people – of any gender – behave in dominating ways or their status goes up, and decrease when people behave in nurturing ways or their status goes down.

SCIENTISTS ACTUALLY FIND MUCH STRONGER EVIDENCE OF SOCIAL BEHAVIORS CHANGING HORMONES THAN HORMONES CHANGING BEHAVIOR.

More conscious interventions also have a physical impact on our bodies or how other people read our gender, such as taking hormones or drugs that impact hormone levels like birth control, steroids, or some cancer treatments; having surgeries like breast reduction or enhancement, genital alterations, hysterectomy or prostatectomy; removing body hair; or wearing items such as bras and binders, make-up, piercings or tattoos.

THROWING LIKE A GIRL

In her classic essay "Throwing like a girl", political theorist Iris Marion Young points out how differently boys and girls are socialized in relation to their bodies. She points out that women don't see themselves as capable, become used to thinking "I can't" rather than "I can", and approach tasks this way.

The fact that it's an insult to do something "like a girl" is part of the wider cultural message girls internalize, as is how they are treated as fragile and encouraged to constantly monitor and control their bodies to avoid embarrassment or unattractiveness. This can gender people into more stereotypically feminine or masculine physiques, behaviour, and beliefs.

If children of all genders were equally encouraged to feel free in their bodies and to believe in their strength and physical capability, what might happen to their bodies, capacities, and potentials over time?

39

DOING GENDER

In the 1980s, sociologists Candace West and Don Zimmerman came up with the idea that gender is something we do: "We perform gender in our interactions with others, and are then judged on how well we fit social norms of gender. So gender is a routine accomplishment embedded in everyday interaction. Gender is 'omnirelevant' because it's prevalent in so many taken-for-granted activities, e.g. bathrooms, sports, sex, conversations, employed work, and the division of labour."

We're rarely conscious of the ways in which we do gender: it's so habitual when we've repeated it over and over again. However, we may become aware of how we're always doing gender when we're judged for doing it "wrong" for a body like ours, or when we consciously try to do it differently.

GENDER PERFORMATIVITY

Gender theorist Judith Butler built on the concept of doing gender with her idea of gender performativity.

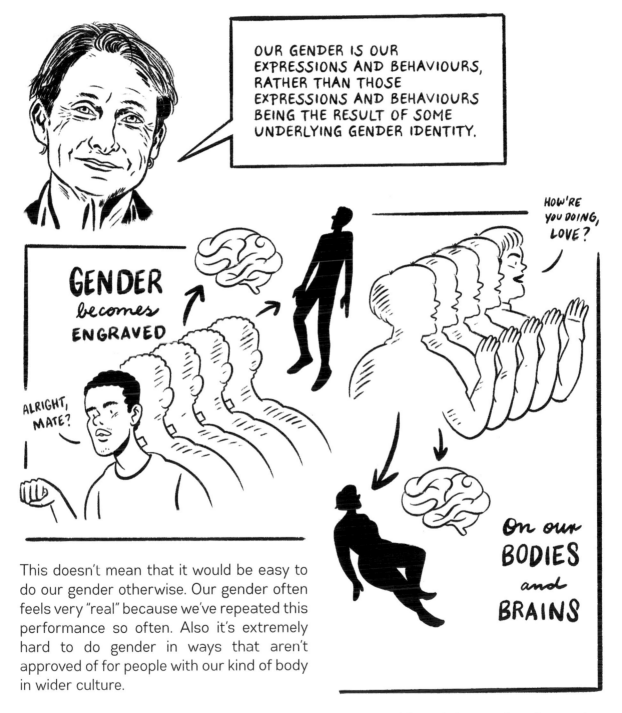

OUR GENDER IS OUR EXPRESSIONS AND BEHAVIOURS, RATHER THAN THOSE EXPRESSIONS AND BEHAVIOURS BEING THE RESULT OF SOME UNDERLYING GENDER IDENTITY.

HOW'RE YOU DOING, LOVE?

GENDER becomes ENGRAVED

ALRIGHT, MATE?

On our BODIES and BRAINS

This doesn't mean that it would be easy to do our gender otherwise. Our gender often feels very "real" because we've repeated this performance so often. Also it's extremely hard to do gender in ways that aren't approved of for people with our kind of body in wider culture.

Our bodies and brains are shaped by the constant repetition of the gendered ways in which we have learnt to speak, to dress, to move through the world, to take up space or not, to express emotion or not, to find pleasure in things, to relate to others, and the myriad other micro-actions we engage in many times a day.

GENDER FLUIDITY

Existential philosopher Simone de Beauvoir famously said: "One is not born but rather becomes a woman."

Our sex/gender can also change based on our resisting this norm and finding alternatives.

WE DON'T SEE MANY SEX DIFFERENCES IN CHILDREN'S BRAINS. MOST START IN ADOLESCENCE OR ADULTHOOD, AND SOME DISAPPEAR AROUND MENOPAUSE OR IN OLD AGE. THESE DIFFERENCES MAY DEPEND ON HORMONE LEVELS OR ENVIRONMENTAL CONDITIONS.

DAPHNA JOEL

As we would expect from what we've covered here, such changes are reflected in our bodies and brains.

LEVELS OF EXPERIENCE

Given that we all grow up in quite a similar gender system – as we saw in Chapter 1 – why are our ways of experiencing, identifying, and expressing our genders so diverse?

One reason is that we're each affected by a unique set of influences. These include the gender options that are available to us in our particular wider culture, but they also include the communities and institutions we're part of, our interpersonal relationships now, and the families we grew up in.

At each of these levels, gender norms might be strongly reinforced, or resisted. We might be presented with very limited options, or a wider range of possibilities. Of course, all these things will shift over time too as our culture, communities, relationships, and experience of ourselves change.

INTERSECTIONAL GENDER

Another reason our experiences of gender are so diverse is because our gender can't be disentangled from other aspects of ourselves like our race, class, sexuality, or disability. We each differ on these aspects in terms of how socially privileged or oppressed we are, and in terms of our lived experience of gender. This idea is known as intersectionality.

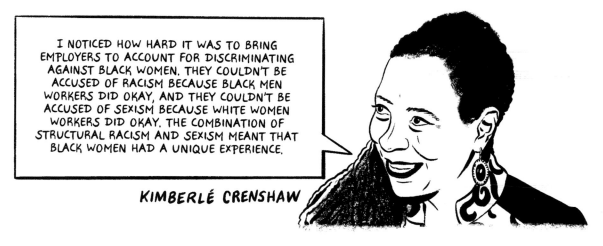

I NOTICED HOW HARD IT WAS TO BRING EMPLOYERS TO ACCOUNT FOR DISCRIMINATING AGAINST BLACK WOMEN. THEY COULDN'T BE ACCUSED OF RACISM BECAUSE BLACK MEN WORKERS DID OKAY, AND THEY COULDN'T BE ACCUSED OF SEXISM BECAUSE WHITE WOMEN WORKERS DID OKAY. THE COMBINATION OF STRUCTURAL RACISM AND SEXISM MEANT THAT BLACK WOMEN HAD A UNIQUE EXPERIENCE.

KIMBERLÉ CRENSHAW

We have diverse experiences of gender because of the gender options that are available to us – or not – at our specific intersectional position – which may also change over time. For example, growing up in a working-class neighbourhood may make some versions of masculinity available, while going to college may offer others. Different ways of expressing femininity may be available before and after developing a chronic health condition.

UNDOING AND TROUBLING GENDER

When the systems and structures of gender around us are so powerful, how much flexibility and freedom do we have to do our gender differently?

Sociologist Tray Yeadon-Lee found that, as well as "doing gender", people also "undo", "redo", and "remake" gender in various ways.

Judith Butler says that we can never step outside the existing power relations completely. We have to repeat gender performance on an everyday basis. But, we can do something different in how we repeat them. We can create gender trouble and subversive confusion through parody or performances of gender which challenge expectations.

SEX/GENDER IS BIOPSYCHOSOCIAL, NON-BINARY, FLUID, AND INTERSECTIONAL

Let's recap:

- Both "sex" and "gender" are used to refer to multiple, often overlapping, aspects of a person.
- On no level is there a simple binary between women and men – sex and gender are more of a spectrum or multiplicity.
- Sex/gender can't be separated into a nature/nurture binary. Instead it is biopsychosocial with all those elements influencing each other.
- Our experience of our own genders doesn't necessarily map onto the assumptions made about our bodies.
- Our experience and expression of gender changes over time, fluidly; we're always in a process of becoming our gender.

The assumption of a nature/nurture binary underlies common debates about whether people are "born" into a sex/gender, whether trans men and women are "really" men and women, and whether certain gender roles are "natural". We can't know which aspects of our gender are down to nature or nurture, but even if we could tease these things apart, it shouldn't affect how we treat people.

We'll return to binaries and fluidity in Chapters 5 and 6.

FEMININITIES, MASCULINITIES, AND NON-BINARY GENDERS

We've now explored how the gender understandings, ideals, and norms in the world around us were formed historically. We've also looked at the complexity of the ways in which they shape our experiences today.

Now let's take a closer look at what those gender understandings, ideals, and norms are.

What masculinities, femininities, and other gender possibilities are available to us in our current time and place?

CHAPTER THREE: MASCULINITIES - MAN AS NORM

In Chapter 1 we (briefly!) explored millennia of patriarchy, particularly the scientific project of the last 100 years or so of categorizing what's "normal", and equating this with "healthy" and "superior".

One legacy of this is the view that (a certain kind of) man is the norm/ideal against which everyone else is defined. We see this in the use of "mankind" and "he" to mean everyone, and the way labels for women are often feminized versions of labels for men.

Exceptions to this are telling: "widow" is a rare word where the male version is a variant on the female, perhaps because women are more defined by their relationships to others. Only studies on parenting tend to present data from women before that from men.

So why are we following suit in this book by presenting masculinities before other genders? We need to understand the supposed norm before we can consider how others are defined in relation to it. Damn you, patriarchy.

MALE PRIVILEGE

Related to the concept of "man as norm", **male privilege** refers to the invisible systems which men benefit from, often unaware that they do so.*

Author Barry Deutsch's male privilege checklist includes experiences like:

As a result of male privilege, many men unconsciously take up more physical and conversational space than others, and/or believe that their bodies, ideas, and labour have greater value and importance.

* This concept was inspired by Peggy McIntosh's work on **white privilege**, which of course intersects with male privilege for white men.

HEGEMONIC MASCULINITY

For decades academic disciplines pretty exclusively centred on men, assuming their experience to be universal, or of singular importance. But academics rarely studied them as men, just as the supposed normal human being.

Only in the last few decades have people begun to study and develop theories about why men are like they are, and how masculinities work (similar developments have occured in the study of whiteness, heterosexuality, etc.).

One of the major figures in this field is Raewyn Connell, who came up with the idea of **hegemonic masculinity.**

THIS IS THE DOMINANT IDEAL FORM OF MASCULINITY WHICH ALL BOYS AND MEN ORGANIZE THEMSELVES IN RELATION TO.

THE IDEALIZED MAN IS YOUNG, MARRIED, WHITE, URBAN, HETEROSEXUAL, FATHER, OF COLLEGE EDUCATION, FULLY EMPLOYED, OF GOOD COMPLEXION, WEIGHT AND HEIGHT, AND WITH A RECENT RECORD IN SPORTS.

SOCIOLOGIST ERVING GOFFMAN

DIMENSIONS OF MASCULINITY

According to psychologists Amy Cohn and Amos Zeichner, there are four key dimensions to hegemonic masculinity:

- COMPETITIVENESS AND DOMINANCE

- EMOTIONAL INEXPRESSIVENESS (the only permissable emotion is anger)

- GENDER ROLE STRESS (the strain of keeping up the act of masculinity)

- HOMOPHOBIA AND MISOGYNY

Linking all these dimensions is the rejection of self-care and help-seeking as "not manly".

THE MASCULINITY PYRAMID

Hegemonic masculinity sits at the top of a hierarchy of other masculinities.

There's a belief that accepting your position in relation to hegemonic masculinity – and keeping to the norms of that position – will help men to meet social expectations of manhood. Any man who fails to qualify in any one of these ways is likely to view himself as unworthy, incomplete, and inferior.

COMPLICIT MASCULINITIES INCLUDE MEN WHO DON'T REACH THE IDEAL BUT FIT MANY OF THE CHARACTERISTICS, SO STILL BENEFIT FROM MALE PRIVILEGE THROUGH THE "PATRIARCHAL DIVIDEND".

SUBORDINATED MASCULINITIES INCLUDE MEN WHO ARE EXCLUDED FROM MASCULINITY IN WIDER CULTURE, SUCH AS GAY MEN, OR MEN PERCEIVED AS FEMININE.

7,715 likes

disgusting

MARGINALIZED MASCULINITIES INCLUDE MEN WHO DON'T RECEIVE ALL THE BENEFITS OF MALE PRIVILEGE DUE TO RACE, CLASS, ETC.

N.W.A.

WORKING-CLASS MEN ARE THE MALE EQUIVALENT OF THE "DUMB BLONDE" - ENDOWED WITH PHYSICAL VIRTUES BUT PROBLEMATIZED BY INTELLECTUAL SHORTCOMINGS.

SOCIOLOGIST-ACTIVIST BETHANY COSTON

53

MULTIPLE MASCULINITIES

We're talking about "masculinities", not "masculinity", because there are clearly many varieties available.

The dominant and other available forms of masculinity differ across time and culture; so our notions of what counts as "masculine" are **socially constructed**, open to being contested, and subject to changing over time.

Social psychologists Margaret Wetherell and Nigel Edley found that men draw on multiple hegemonic and complicit masculinities when they talk about themselves. They also enact masculinity differently in different situations, like work, school, or home.

It's important to remember though that not all masculinities are equally available to everyone. Only men of a certain class, race, sexuality, and body can claim or express hegemonic and complicit masculinities. Different situations can expand or limit the masculinities which can be expressed.

"NOT GAY": HOMOPHOBIA, MISOGYNY, AND MASCULINITY

Many authors have pointed out that masculinity is also defined in opposition to femininity and gayness. The performance of hetero masculinity often involves distancing from those qualities through teasing and/or overt homophobia and misogyny.

THE CONTRADICTION OF HEGEMONIC MASCULINITY IS THAT MANY STRAIGHT WHITE MEN DO ENGAGE IN CLOSE BONDING, AND SEX, WITH OTHER MEN, WHILE REJECTING GAYNESS. THIS INCLUDES HOOKING UP WITH OTHER MEN FOR SEX, AND FRATERNITY AND MILITARY HAZING RITUALS WHERE NEW RECRUITS ARE MADE TO GRAB EACH OTHER'S PENISES AND STICK FINGERS UP THEIR FELLOW MEMBERS' ANUSES.

PROFESSOR OF GENDER AND SEXUALITY STUDIES **JANE WARD**

I'M STILL STRAIGHT.

'COURSE, ME TOO. FANCY A BRO JOB?

GAY MASCULINITIES AND FEMININITY

Subordinated and marginalized masculinities don't escape from this distancing from anything regarded as feminine.

Some gay men also replicate straight men's misogyny, acting entitled to touch or comment upon women's bodies.

TOXIC MASCULINITY

Toxic masculinity is the idea that it is damaging to everyone when men endeavour to meet the ideals of masculinity: dominance, misogyny/homophobia, and repression of emotions except anger.

The idea of toxic masculinity doesn't aim to demonize men, but to emphasize the harmful effects of conforming to ideal masculine behaviors. The normalization of violence, non-consent, entitlement, and power over others is implicated in domestic violence, sexual assault, and hate-crimes.

THE BOY CODE IS LEARNT FROM A YOUNG AGE, THROUGH SOCIALIZATION THAT BOYS MUST REJECT ANYTHING PERCEIVED AS "FEMININE".

PSYCHOLOGIST STEPHEN FROSH

LITTLE TERROR

THESE!

Ladies' MAN

NOT THOSE

WONDER WOMAN

KING OF THE CASTLE

SUPER HERO IN TRAINING

TOXIC FOR WHOM? THE "CRISIS OF MASCULINITY"

Toxic masculinity is bad for those who men hurt, but it's also bad for men themselves as it stifles emotions and insists on self-reliance. It's bad for wider society in the "masculinist" systems and dynamics it perpetuates: families, institutions, communities, and politics based on hegemonic masculine ideals such as hiding emotions, competitiveness, and lack of care for self or others.

We might also have heard the common idea that masculinity is in crisis. This describes a double bind in which men try to meet old standards of masculinity in a world which is going through changes in:

• **Work** – which means that many men are unemployed or in jobs where ideals of masculinity are not valued.
• **The family** – which means that men are no longer necessarily breadwinners or heads of household.

Such challenges to masculine identity have been linked to the high rates of suicide, addiction, and physical health problems in men.

FRAGILE MASCULINITIES

The idea of **fragile masculinity** points to how men are hailed in hypermasculine ways to reassure them of their manliness. This happens because of how precarious maintaining the performance of masculinity can be, especially under the "crisis of masculinity". However, the whole concept of the crisis of masculinity has been criticized for treating men as one homogenous group, and for the way it gets deployed as part of a backlash against feminism and gender equality.

Pointing out the fragility of masculinity is one way of advocating for a change in the masculine norm.

MASCULINITY AND VIOLENCE

Men are much more likely than women to be both perpetrators and victims of violence. Non-consensual behaviour from men has often been linked to the alienation and the violence they are encouraged to do to themselves in performing masculinity.

bell hooks

SHOWING AGGRESSION IS THE SIMPLEST WAY TO ASSERT PATRIARCHAL MANHOOD. ALL MEN MUST DEMONSTRATE THAT THEY ARE CAPABLE OF BEING VIOLENT.

JUVIE!

Despite being encouraged into demonstrating violence, men are generally held more responsible and criminalized for it. When women demonstrate these same behaviours, they're more likely to be regarded as victims, and pathologized. Men tend to be seen as "bad", and women as "mad" because men are regarded as having more agency than woman.

RACE AND MASCULINITY

It is vital to be mindful of the intersection between gender and race here. The stereotype of the violent black man in mainstream culture has a huge impact on which men tend to be most criminalized, and which crimes punished most harshly.

ACADEMIC-ACTIVIST ORNETTE D. CLENNON

THE IMAGE OF BLACK MEN AS HYPERMASCULINE CAN ALSO BECOME A CULTURAL TOOL OF SELF-REGULATION AND SELF-LOATHING.

Many white men perform masculinity by "othering" different racial groups (as well as women and gay men).

THE ANGER OF WHITE MEN CAN BE LINKED TO THE CULTURAL PROMISE THAT THEY CAN BE ANYTHING AND HAVE ANYTHING, AND THE SENSE THAT THEY'VE HAD THAT FUTURE TAKEN AWAY FROM THEM.

AUTHOR OF <u>SO YOU WANT TO TALK ABOUT RACE</u>, IJEOMA OLUO

I WOULD HAVE MY DREAM JOB IF IT WEREN'T FOR POLITICALLY CORRECT HIRING POLICIES.

MASCULINITY AND SHAME

Psychologists Michael Beattie and Penny Lenihan point out that men's anger can also be linked to shame: the socialization that men should be able to handle everything that happens to them alone can lead to feelings of inadequacy when they inevitably can't.

Therapists David Shepard & Fredric Rabinowitz suggest that men are in a triple bind. They are shamed by each other into normative masculine behaviour, including hiding normal emotional expression. That shaming creates the potential for rage, a desire to hide, and a sense of poor self worth, none of which can be talked about or dealt with since another aspect of orthodox masculine gender performance involves a prohibition on help-seeking.

WRITER ROBERT KAZANDJIAN

LEARNING TO PERFORM MY MASCULINITY I UNDERSTOOD THAT I WAS SUPPOSED TO SWALLOW DISAPPOINTMENT AND SADNESS, LET IT SWIRL INTO ANGER, AND THEN SPIT IT BACK OUT LIKE DRAGON FIRE.

NEW MEN AND METROSEXUALS

In recent decades, attention has turned to **reconstructed masculinities** that challenge – or offer alternatives to – hegemonic masculinity as well as to **unreconstructed masculinities** that nostalgically and/or ironically cling on to them.

The "new man" of the 1980s rejected misogyny and aggression, believed in equality of domestic labour and childcare, and was emotionally sensitive.

DAVID BECKHAM

In the 1990s and 2000s Mark Simpson coined the term "metrosexual" for single young men of any sexuality who had a high disposable income and were concerned with physical appearance: fashion, grooming, working out, etc. Their narcissistic love/sex interest in themselves – as men – differentiated them from culturally dominant masculine codes. "Spornosexual" and "hipster" are more recent terms for versions of metrosexuality. The masculine ideal has shifted to focus on appearance, due to the decline of manual labour, which had enabled a certain kind of physique along with paid work. There has been resistance to such new masculinities in places that historically relied more on such labour.

INCLUSIVE MASCULINITIES

Eric Anderson and Mark McCormack's studies of school and college students in the US and UK suggest a shift to peers valuing more inclusive masculinities which undermine old values of homophobia and misogyny. We see this represented in "bromance" movies and TV shows like *Brooklyn 99* and *Lovesick* which show physical and emotional intimacy between men.

However, other intersections like class and geographical location impact whether inclusive masculinities are available to boys and men across different contexts. More inclusive masculinities also don't necessarily challenge gendered power dynamics and inequalities which disadvantage women.

BACKLASH MASCULINITIES: LADS

There has also been backlash against new inclusive masculinities, often with a return to more hegemonic values. For example, media scholar David Gauntlett writes that "new lads" in the UK (like fraternity culture in the US) were a 1990s reaction to the "new man" and "girl power" postfeminism. Associated with Britpop, comedy, and lads' magazines, they returned to male bonding through misogynist, homophobic, and racist "banter", but with a claim that this was all knowing ironic humour, which made it difficult to challenge. However, lads' mags did sometimes open up a space - within the safe container of laddism - for more vulnerable conversations about bodies, relationships, and insecurities.

This kind of lad culture continues, particularly in marketing to young men in colleges and universities, such as ads that include sexualized images of young women passed out or labelled "jailbait" and incentives for women to strip or get drunk.

BACKLASH MASCULINITIES: SEDUCTION

The seduction community is a movement of men who teach and share techniques for having sex with women, including persuasion and overcoming resistance.

Ethnographer Rachel O'Neill studied the multi-million dollar seduction industry and found that it frames sex and relationships as something that men need to work on by attending training and paying for coaching. This can take men further away from intimacy, as they're encouraged to continually, compulsively chase mastery of the seduction of women (as something done to them) rather than relating with women. This perpetuates the gender power dynamics that make relationships between men and women more distant, cause problems for men's mental health, and limit the potential for mutual consensual sex and relationships.

> YOU'RE FAILING BECAUSE YOU KEEP WONDERING WHAT WOMEN WANT. IT'S TIME TO FOCUS ON GETTING WHAT *YOU* WANT.

> WOMEN WANT A MAN WHO'LL PROVIDE FOR THEM, NOT SOMEONE TO TALK TO ABOUT THEIR FEELINGS.

> MEN ARE MORE LIKELY TO BE VICTIMS OF HOMICIDE, DEATH IN CONFLICT, DEATH AT WORK. THEY GET LONGER PRISON SENTENCES AND DON'T GET CHILD CUSTODY. THE IDEA OF "MALE PRIVILEGE" IS A FEMINIST CONSPIRACY.

MEN'S ♂ RIGHTS

Retrosexuals, Men's Rights Activists (MRAs), and meninists are further examples of backlash masculinities.

GEEK MASCULINITIES

Geek masculinities may seem like a shift away from hegemonic masculinities given they often value smarts and being a "nice guy" instead of physical strength or macho dominance.

Author Laurie Penny points out that geek masculinity is dangerous because nerd guys often went through bullying and trauma in their early lives. This can leave them with a sense of entitlement to good things now, blinker them to their current privilege, and make them disinclined to believe that others may have had it even worse than them because their trauma was compounded by structural oppression.

Geek masculinities also include **incels** (involuntary celibates) and **beta males**. The **manosphere** refers to parts of the internet where such men - as well a MRAs and PUAs - meet. Many adhere to **"red pill"** philosophies that blame women and/or feminism for their suffering rather than hegemonic masculinity.

REVENGE OF THE NERDS?

GEEK MASCULINITY BECAME PART OF POPULAR CULTURE WITH SHOWS LIKE THE BIG BANG THEORY, THE MOST-WATCHED SHOW ON TV. IT DEMONSTRATES THE COMPLICITY OF NERDY "NICE GUYS" IN ENTITLED TOXIC MASCULINITY AND IN REINFORCING HEGEMONIC MASCULINITY. FRAMING MISOGYNY AS "ADORKABLE" LETS GEEK GUYS OFF THE HOOK FOR SEXIST AND NON-CONSENSUAL BEHAVIOUR.

CULTURAL CRITIC AND CREATOR OF YOUTUBE'S "POP CULTURE DETECTIVE AGENCY", JONATHAN McINTOSH

FIRST WE LET THE LAWYERS AND THE JOCKS THIN THE HERD, AND THEN WE GO AFTER THE WEAK AND THE OLD AND THE LAME.

A GIRLS NIGHT IN? OH I DON'T KNOW IF I'M UP FOR AN EVENING TALKING ABOUT RAINBOWS, UNICORNS, AND MENSTRUAL CRAMPS.

Like the "irony" of lad culture, such shows use **lampshade hanging** where they demonstrate awareness of offensive stereotypes in order to get away with using them for laughs anyway.

EXPANDING AVAILABLE MASCULINITIES

As we saw on p.54, boys and men draw on both the dominant and other available forms of masculinity (and sometimes femininities and non-binary gender expressions too) to shape their own gender identities and expressions. Available forms of masculinity shift and change over time and by geographical location. Men often draw on multiple different masculinities across different times and contexts.

Some masculinities challenge all the dimensions of hegemonic masculinity. However, most are still steeped in white, middle-class values. They tend to minimize the role of structural oppression and adhere to a **neoliberal,** individualistic view that we live in a time of equality where anyone can do well.

POSTFEMINIST MASCULINITIES

While men embracing feminism is obviously to be encouraged, it can be done in ways that fail to shift their behaviours - or wider gender dynamics - as profoundly as they might.

CELEBRITY FEMINIST MEN OFTEN PRESENT A RATIONAL, LIBERAL KIND OF FEMINISM. THIS CAN SUGGEST THAT FEMINIST WOMEN ARE TOO EMOTIONAL AND POLITICAL IN THE WAY THEY EXPRESS THEIR VIEWS, SO FEMINIST MEN ARE REQUIRED TO DO IT FOR THEM.

WHEN CELEB FEMINIST MEN BECOME FATHERS THEY'RE OFTEN REGARDED AS SEXY AND FEMINIST, WHILE OFTEN REMAINING COMPLICIT IN GENDERED DIVISIONS OF DOMESTIC LABOUR.

MEDIA SCHOLAR HANNAH HAMAD

Hey, girl. It's okay. Thinking about the greed of Major Corporations makes me cry, too

31 PHOTOS OF HOT GUYS WITH BABIES GUARANTEED TO MAKE YOU SWOON

RYAN GOSLING THANKS WIFE FOR STEPPING OUT OF THE PUBLIC SPHERE TO LOOK AFTER KIDS

GENTLE MEN

If further forms of masculinity are represented in popular culture, they may become available for more men to draw upon. For example, the 2018 TV show *Queer Eye* opens up the idea that – across intersections of race, class, faith, and sexuality – if guys are to be happy and fulfilled, they need to open up emotionally, express their vulnerability, and connect with others.

TENDER MASCULINITIES

Feminist journalist Terra Loire coined the term "tender masculinities" to capture representations which provide an alternative to both macho men and "nice guys".

Loire's checklist of how to spot a tender man includes: Is he invested in all his relationships, not just romantic/sexual ones? Does he express his emotions? Is he self-aware? Is he committed to personal growth? Does he respect boundaries? Is he unafraid of intimacy with other men?

MASCULINITIES BEYOND MEN

In Chapter 2 we covered the shift from the common idea of gender as innate, to gender as something we draw upon from the world around us to shape our own identity, expression, and experience, biopsychosocially.

These masculinities (and other gender expressions) are available to all of us – all genders can draw upon and perform them. The same goes for femininities and non-binary genders, which we'll look at in the next chapters.

THE DRAG KING BOOK

CN LESTER

SAMIRA WILEY & LEA DELARIA

This is why we need to be cautious with terms like "men's studies" or "men's movement": masculinities are not only about men.

FEMALE MASCULINITIES

In the queer theory book *Female Masculinity*, Jack Halberstam takes aim at the protected status of male masculinity and shows that female masculinity has offered a distinct alternative to it for well over 200 years.

We seem to be comfortable with masculinity on a female body in young tomboys. It only becomes threatening when that masculinity is still apparent as the child heads into adolescence. We also tend to see arguments about "excessive masculinity" focused on black, Latinx or working-class bodies (of any gender).

BUTCH

One common conception of female masculinity is "butch", a term that has been used to refer to masculine women, particularly in lesbian communities.

WRITER LAURA BRIDGEMAN

IN THE BUTCH MONOLOGUES WE EXPLORE DIVERSE EXPERIENCES OF BUTCHNESS ACROSS CIS WOMEN, NON-BINARY PEOPLE, AND TRANS FOLKS, AND THE RADICAL CHALLENGES THESE CAN POSE TO CONVENTIONAL MASCULINITIES.

DIRECTOR JULIE McNAMARA

The Butch Monologues performance challenges the idea that people need to tell singular, static narratives about their masculinities, and reminds us how masculinities intersect with race, class, age, generation, disability, and geographical location.

HOW CAN WE SHIFT MASCULINITY?

Theories of masculinity don't make much difference if they're only known by academics. Sex and relationships educator Justin Hancock created this model to explain to men and boys how masculinity works.

Understanding the impact of this way of doing masculinity, and *changing it*, is vital. We could, for instance, encourage masculinities that emphasize men talking with other men about their feelings.

CHAPTER FOUR: FEMININITIES & FEMINISMS

As with masculinity, there are many forms of femininity, not just one. Women (and others) draw on the forms of femininity that are available in the world around them. Also, dominant - or hegemonic - forms of femininity shape everyone's experience. These are generally focused on young, white, middle-class, non-disabled, heterosexual, and thin women.

However, because femininity is defined in relation to a supposed masculine norm of humanity, even dominant forms of femininity are still subordinate to masculinity.

In this Chapter we'll explore how various waves of feminism have shaped which forms of femininity are available, as well as in challenging "men as norm" assumptions. Let's start by unpacking that a little more ...

1ST WAVE

2ND WAVE

POLICE BOX

3RD WAVE

MY FEMINISM WILL BE INTERSECTIONAL OR IT WILL BE BULLSHIT!

4TH WAVE

TARANA BURKE

100 MOST INFLUENTIAL PEOPLE

WOMAN AS "OTHER"

In *The Second Sex*, existential philosopher Simone de Beauvoir presents the idea of woman as "other": meaning that women are defined as what men are not.

IT'S POSSIBLE FOR MEN TO BE FREE TO BE "FOR-THEMSELVES" WHEREAS WOMEN MUST BE "FOR-OTHERS": DUTIFUL DAUGHTERS, DESIRABLE WOMEN, WIVES, AND MOTHERS.

Art critic John Berger highlights this dichotomy in media representations when he says "men act and women appear": men look at women. Women watch themselves being looked at.

Film theorist Laura Mulvey points out that women audiences have to view themselves through the **male gaze**, because the camera puts the audience in the place of a heterosexual man.

Women still have only a third of the lines in Hollywood movies, because men have been assumed to be the standard of humanity that audiences will relate to, and so they make up the vast majority of main characters. Most movies still fail cartoonist Alison Bechdel's test for whether films represent women as humans in their own right:

The view of women as "other" or inferior has implications for the ways in which women's labour and bodies are valued. Around the world, women earn 20% less than men, and up to 70% of women have experienced physical and/or sexual violence from an intimate partner.

FEMALE PRIVILEGE

Some have attempted to create female privilege checklists along the lines of the male privilege checklist, including experiences like:

Such "privileges" are debatable given that they fail to take into account the history of patriarchal power structures.

PROBLEMS WITH FEMALE PRIVILEGE

These kinds of "female privilege" are often rooted in being regarded as less human, adult, responsible, and agentic than men, as well as being defined by relationships with others.

While women who transgress the rules of society may be treated more leniently than men, women who transgress the rules of femininity in addition to the rules of society are generally treated much more harshly and viewed as monstrous, or even supernatural (as we'll see in a few pages). This includes violent, non-maternal, or sexual women.

It's also vital to think intersectionally here because only certain women (and men) are afforded the "privileges" on these checklists.

HEGEMONIC FEMININITIES

Raewyn Connell doesn't think that there's such a thing as hegemonic femininity – in the same way there is for masculinity – because all forms of femininity develop in the context of the overall subordination of women to men. No form of femininity holds the same position among women that hegemonic masculinity does among men.

Sociologist Mimi Schippers argues that there is such a thing as hegemonic femininity because there are forms of femininity which are privileged over others and which serve the dominant gender order, and men's domination.

PARIAH FEMININITIES

PARIAH FEMININITIES ARE THOSE PRACTICES AND CHARACTERISTICS EMBODIED BY WOMEN THAT REFUSE TO COMPLEMENT HEGEMONIC MASCULINITY AND THEREFORE THREATEN MALE DOMINANCE.

MIMI SCHIPPERS

NO MEANS NO.

HAVING SEXUAL DESIRE FOR OTHER WOMEN

BEING EITHER PROMISCUOUS OR SEXUALLY INACCESSIBLE

BEING AGGRESSIVE

SELFISHNESS COULD BE SEEN AS ANOTHER FORM OF PARIAH FEMININITY. "SELFISH" WOMEN ARE VILIFIED AS PARTICULARLY DEVIANT AND/OR MASCULINE. THE STEREOTYPE OF BEING NATURALLY PREDISPOSED TOWARDS COLLABORATION, CARING, AND COMMUNITY IS AN STRAITJACKET FOR WOMEN.

PROFESSOR OF SOCIOLOGY LISA DOWNING

Historically women have been demonized as witches if they were old; unattractive to men; not maternal or child-bearing; wise, smart, or powerful; and/or independent and unreliant on men.

TOXIC FEMININITY?

Is there such a thing as toxic femininity? As with female privilege and hegemonic femininity, it's an arguable concept in the face of global and historical patriarchal oppression.

However, we might propose that femininity is toxic when it assumes that – by virtue of being feminine – it is impossible for women to cause harm. This may be because women are regarded as having no agency. Or it may be because when women have themselves been oppressed or abused, it is unbearable to recognize their own culpability in the oppression or abuse of others.

TOXIC FEMININITY AND INTERSECTIONALITY

Author Luvvie Ajayi suggests that femininity can become toxic when women lack awareness of:

- INTERSECTING POWER STRUCTURES OTHER THAN GENDER (e.g. AGE, CLASS, RACE, GENDER STATUS), AND
- THE MULTIPLE (LESS VISIBLE) FORMS THAT VIOLENCE CAN TAKE BEYOND PHYSICAL AND SEXUAL, LIKE SYMBOLIC VIOLENCE WHERE DOMINANT GROUPS IMPOSE THEIR IDEOLOGY ON OTHERS TO MAKE THE STATUS QUO SEEM LEGITIMATE AND NATURAL.

LIKE, I JUST FEEL VERY ATTACKED, LIKE YOU'RE BEING SO CONFLICTUAL RIGHT NOW.

An example of toxic femininity that intersects with race marginalization is what journalist Ruby Hamad calls "White women tears". This is when those women who are afforded the most protection in society - and are seen as the prototype of womanhood - fail to acknowledge either the additional burdens that women of colour bear, or their own complicity in maintaining the racial status quo.

WHEN BLACK AND BROWN WOMEN ATTEMPT TO CONFRONT WHITE WOMEN ABOUT SOMETHING THEY'VE DONE THAT'S IMPACTED THEM ADVERSELY, THEY'RE OFTEN MET WITH TEARFUL DENIALS AND INDIGNANT ACCUSATIONS THAT THEY'RE THE ONE WHO HAS BEEN HURT – PAINTING THE BLACK OR BROWN WOMAN AS THE AGGRESSOR, AND DENYING THEM A VOICE.

RUBY HAMAD

MULTIPLE FEMININITIES AND FEMINISM

Shifting understandings of gender over time have made different versions of femininity available, some of which challenge hegemonic femininities. In particular the different waves of feminism have expanded (and contracted) which femininties are available.

LATE 1800s - EARLY 1900s
FIRST WAVE ~
SUFFRAGE: FIGHTING
FOR VOTES

1960s - 1970s
SECOND WAVE ~ WOMEN'S
LIBERATION MOVEMENTS:
FIGHTING FOR GENDER EQUALITY

1980s ~
CRITIQUES AND
SPLITS IN THE WOMEN'S
MOVEMENT

1990s ONWARDS ~
POSTFEMINIST BACKLASH
AGAINST FEMINISM

2000s ONWARDS
THIRD WAVE ~ MORE
INTERSECTIONAL FEMINISM

2012 ONWARDS
FOURTH WAVE ~
SOCIAL MEDIA
FEMINISM

FIRST-WAVE FEMINISM

The first wave of feminism largely focused on obtaining votes for women. It opened up the possibility for women to see themselves as citizens.

However, the movement was largely white and middle-class in most countries, meaning that working-class women and women of colour were excluded, or treated as inferior or in need of saving. Also, many suffrage arguments were based on the idea that women were "naturally" kinder, more "civilized", and suited to caring roles, which limited the available femininities.

LOOK AT ME! LOOK AT MY ARM! I HAVE PLOUGHED, AND PLANTED, AND GATHERED INTO BARNS, AND NO MAN COULD HEAD ME! AND AIN'T I A WOMAN?

AFRICAN AMERICAN ABOLITIONIST & WOMEN'S RIGHTS ACTIVIST SOJOURNER TRUTH, 1851

If Truth's ideas had been incorporated into the first wave of mainstream feminism they would have enabled some very different understandings and expressions of femininity.

SECOND-WAVE FEMINISM

During WWII, in many countries women worked in factories and in the military, which opened up wider understandings of what women were capable of and thus what was possible within femininity. However, in many places this closed down after the war. As women returned to the home, femininity returned to being associated with domesticity.

The second wave of feminism arose out of frustration with post-war limitations, spawning a social movement in the 1960s and 70s which called for cultural - as much as economic or political - change. Feminists like Betty Friedan and Betty Dodson campaigned for equal pay, freedom from discrimination, and the rights to define your own sexuality and to be free from violence.

A major limitation of second-wave feminism, as with the first wave, was that it centred on white middle-class women as if they were the universal woman.

BLACK FEMINIST CRITIQUES AND FEMINIST FRAGMENTATIONS

YOU'RE FIGHTING FOR THE RIGHT TO WORK OUTSIDE THE HOME, BUT WE'VE BEEN DOING IT FOR YEARS — OFTEN IN YOUR HOMES!

As with Sojourner Truth in the 1850s, black feminists in the 60s and 70s provided alternatives to white second-wave feminism, which opened up different possible understandings and expressions of femininity, but which were rarely taken up by mainstream feminism.

A WOMANIST IS A WOMAN WHO LOVES ANOTHER WOMAN, SEXUALLY AND/ OR NON-SEXUALLY. SHE PREFERS WOMEN'S CULTURE AND EMOTIONAL FLEXIBILITY. SHE IS COMMITTED TO THE SURVIVAL AND WHOLENESS OF AN ENTIRE PEOPLE. SHE LOVES HERSELF.

AUTHOR & ACTIVIST ALICE WALKER

I AM NOT FREE WHILE ANY WOMAN IS UNFREE, EVEN WHEN HER SHACKLES ARE VERY DIFFERENT FROM MY OWN ... REACH DOWN INTO THAT DEEP PLACE OF KNOWLEDGE INSIDE YOURSELF AND TOUCH THAT TERROR AND LOATHING OF ANY DIFFERENCE THAT LIVES THERE. SEE WHOSE FACE IT WEARS. THEN THE "PERSONAL AS THE POLITICAL" CAN BEGIN TO ILLUMINATE ALL OUR CHOICES.

BLACK FEMINIST AUDRE LORDE

STRUCTURE/AGENCY AND THE SEX WARS

Second-wave feminists argued that some women needed to have their consciousnesses raised because they didn't realize how much their behaviours were the result of patriarchal oppression.

This created a structure/agency tension that has dogged feminism ever since: Which of us are free agents and which of us are dupes of patriarchal structures? Who gets to judge which femininities are good or bad, feminist or not feminist?

Such issues became key tensions in the feminist "sex wars" of the 1980s, which continue in various forms to this day, and which expanded – and limited – ways of doing sexuality in relation to femininity. For example, "anti-porn" feminists argued that porn is bad for women because it overwhelmingly represents male pleasure and female subservience; that sex work exploits women for male benefit; and that we can't engage with these without supporting patriarchal oppression of women. "Sex-positive" feminists argued that any hierarchy which says one form of sex is better than another should be critiqued. They argued against censorship and that other media are just as problematic as porn.

POSTFEMINISM

Postfeminism, which began around the 1990s, assumes that gender equality had been reached, and even that feminism has gone too far at the expense of men.

As gender scholars Rosalind Gill and Christina Scharff note, it opens up new femininities based around the belief that girls and women have choice and power.

However, postfeminist claims for empowerment and agency often deny structural forces or external influences that limit choice and agency, obscuring the fact that "successful femininity" is young, middle-class, heterosexual, and white, and conforms to restrictive beauty ideals which exclude many women of colour, fat, disabled, and trans women.

The idea that behaviours like dieting, shopping, and pampering are freely chosen and empowering can make them much harder to see in their social context.

THIRD-WAVE FEMINISM

Since the 2000s, third-wave feminism has distanced itself from both the older generation of feminism and apolitical postfeminism. Through grrrl power, artistic performance, irony, rage, and humour, it aims to destabilize gender norms and to challenge sexist practices in everyday life.

For example, slut walks reclaim the word "slut" to draw attention to the sexual double standard and victim-blaming inherent in wider culture. Pussy Riot use punk to protest religious patriarchy and the Putin regime.

Third-wave feminism contains a sense of diverse femininities in coalition rather than a universal femininity.

THE TV SHOW GIRLS PRESENTS REALISTIC FEMININE SEXUALITY AND BODIES, BUT IT'S REALLY WHITE AND INDIVIDUALISTIC.

YEAH, THE SHOW'S CREATOR GOT HAILED AS "THE VOICE OF A GENERATION" WHICH SHOWED HOW NARROW THE WHOLE MEDIA'S OUTLOOK WAS.

Like postfeminism, the third wave has been critiqued for being overly individualist, and for embracing "girliness" and "raunch" in ways that don't pay enough attention to the patriarchal history of the infantilization and sexualization of women.

MY FEMINISM WILL BE INTERSECTIONAL OR IT WILL BE BULLSHIT!

WRITER & BLOGGER FLAVIA DZODAN

One thing that marks the third wave is a more intersectional approach, recognizing the impact of interwoven axes of power and privilege. As we've seen, this approach has been present since before the first wave, but was rarely taken up by mainstream feminism and is often erased from history. Many have spoken against feminism's continued white, middle-class focus.

Alicia Garza, of Black Lives Matter, criticized the women's marches that took place across North America in 2017 and '18 for the marchers' failure to include - or get angry about - injustices against black women (and men).

WHERE WERE ALL OF THESE WHITE PEOPLE WHILE BLACK PEOPLE WERE BEING KILLED IN THE STREETS, JOBLESS, HOMELESS, OVER-INCARCERATED, UNDEREDUCATED?

BRITISH DISCOURSE ON RACE IS WARPED BEYOND LOGIC. FEMINISM IS NOT IMMUNE TO THIS. EVERY MEANINGFUL DISCUSSION ABOUT RACE CENTRES ON WHITE FEELINGS INSTEAD OF BLACK TRUTH. I CAN'T TELL YOU THE AMOUNT OF TIMES I'VE BEEN ACCUSED OF RACISM AGAINST WHITE PEOPLE FOR DARING TO DISCUSS THE CONSEQUENCES OF A WHITE-DOMINATED POLITICAL ATMOSPHERE.

WRITER RENI EDDO-LODGE

INTERWOVEN AXES OF OPPRESSION

Given that oppressive societal structures are interwoven, we have to address all of them to achieve justice, not just the ones that (obviously) affect us personally.

Fat activist Stacy Bias highlights how fat is a feminist issue. Flying while fat is a useful analogy for what needs to happen with many oppressions: instead of designing and occupying our world as if everyone were – or should be – thin, white, non-disabled, affluent, and male, we need to be mindful of the needs of diverse bodies and people.

POSTCOLONIAL FEMINISM

Linked to intersectional feminism, postcolonial feminism criticizes Western feminism for generalizing about women's oppression from a Western perspective:

- Seeing women from non-Western countries as all having identical experiences, and as having the same goals as Westerners
- Denying non-Western women agency and going in as "saviours" to rescue them
- Assuming all women suffer the same kind of patriarchal oppression in the same ways and have the same values and responses to it.

CULTURAL CRITIC
SHIRA TARRANT

EVEN THE IDEA OF WAVES OF FEMINISM IS ANGLOCENTRIC AND BASED ON WHAT HAPPENED IN THE US PRIMARILY.

In Western feminism, "traditional" cultures are frequently presented as sexist and homophobic while "modern" (read: white, Western) cultures are presented as accepting and forward-thinking. The continued sexism and homophobia in "modern" societies is often projected onto "traditional" cultures.

DECOLONIZING FEMINISM

Many intersectional feminists are working to decolonize feminism by examining the impact of colonization on gender understandings. They draw on the work of feminists across the globe instead of focusing on white Western scholars. They explore the cultural meanings of gendered practices rather than imposing Western meanings.

For instance, cultural studies academic Carolyn Pedwell notes the mistake many people make in trying to compare Muslim women wearing headscarves and Western women wearing sexualized (porno chic) clothing, as if both oppress women in similar ways. This fails to recognize the multiple meanings of both practices.

SUCH A VIEW TAKES THE SUPPOSEDLY OPPRESSIVE NATURE OF "NON-WESTERN" PRACTICES FOR GRANTED. THE ASSUMPTION IS THAT "VEILING" IS RELATED TO RACE AND THAT PORNO CHIC IS NOT, AND A DIVIDE IS REINFORCED BETWEEN "WESTERN" AND "NON-WESTERN" PRACTICES WHICH FAILS TO RECOGNIZE THOSE WHO STRADDLE OR TRANSCEND THESE BOUNDARIES.

VS.

Back to structure and agency, it's important to resist the polarization of any women into either cultural dupes, passively taking on board the messages which circulate around them, or the autonomous, agentic and empowered subjects of neo-liberalism, completely free to create themselves in whatever ways they wish.

FOURTH-WAVE FEMINISM?

Some thinkers argue that a fourth wave of feminism began around 2010, thanks to social media: both as a cultural force with its own pressures on women, and as a platform by which feminist discourse is developing, in previously unforeseen ways. Social media allows women to share experiences with new and much larger audiences, such as during the Arab Uprising revolutions, or by calling attention to personal experiences as part of a broader social picture - as in the Everyday Sexism project.

Some commentators argue that different technology doesn't constitute the kind of philosophical shift that happened in each previous wave of feminism and that the "fourth wave" simply means using technology to bring people together around third-wave ideas like intersectionality, privilege, or microaggressions.

Others critique the way feminism can become just part of an individual brand on social media with little sense of collective responsibility or understanding of what has been learnt from prior waves of feminism.

#METOO

One of the most important feminist moments on social media has been #MeToo - a movement founded by campaigner Tarana Burke, which went viral after it got picked up by Hollywood actors calling out their experiences of sexual harassment. The sharing of #MeToo posts made it clear just how common such abuse and assault is, and enabled many to tell their stories for the first time. This led to the exposure of sexual abusers and harassers whose behaviour had previously gone unchallenged.

Sexual assault and abuse is highly gendered, so the focus on female survivors and male perpetrators makes sense. However it can erase the way power dynamics also make other marginalized groups particularly vulnerable to abuse. The "carceral feminist" response of turning to the criminal justice system ignores its inherent structural oppression that makes engagement with it dangerous, for example, for survivors who are people of colour, immigrants, poor, queer, or sex workers.

ANTI-FEMINISM AND NEW MISOGYNIES

Social media has also given a loud voice to the kind of anti-feminist backlash we explored earlier. This shapes which femininities are available, to whom, and how they can be (safely) expressed.

Women who speak out are scrutinized to a degree that men aren't, frequently in relation to their appearance, sexuality, and personal life. They're often subject to trolling in the form of rape and death threats. In an online survey across eight countries, Amnesty International found that over 3/4 of women and girls expect violence and abuse if they express an opinion online.

WHAT TROLLS SAY - AND HOW THEY SAY IT - IS ONLY AN EXTREME VERSION OF WHAT GOES ON ALL THE TIME IN WIDER CULTURE, FOR EXAMPLE IN SENSATIONALIST MEDIA REPORTING. IT'S IMPORTANT TO EXAMINE GENDERED CULTURES OF NON-CONSENT, BULLYING, AND SHAMING, RATHER THAN FOCUSING ON THE "DEVIANT" BEHAVIOUR OF A FEW.

MEDIA SCHOLAR WHITNEY PHILLIPS

@▆▆▆: ugly bitch watch out i know where u live

die

Donald J. Trump
@realDonaldTrump

"@▆▆▆▆▆: If Hillary Clinton can't satisfy her husband what makes her think she can satisfy America?" @realDonaldTrump #2016president"

4/16/15, 5:22 PM

NEW YORK POST

NO WONDER BILL'S AFRAID

Hillary explodes with rage at Benghazi hearing

EMOTIONAL LABOUR AND FEMINIST KILLJOYS

Feminists have turned their attention to how emotions operate in gendered ways, and the impact of this on available femininities. Because emotional expression, self-care, and help-seeking are not regarded as manly under hegemonic masculinity, women are often put in the position of doing emotional work on behalf of men. Jobs involving "**emotional labour**" are undervalued and regarded as feminine. Sociologist Arlie Hochschild came up with this term to describe how employees are often required to make themselves feel and/or express "positive" emotions to invoke positive emotional states in others.

Emotion work, the suppression or expression of particular emotions, is also expected of women at home, in everything from being the one to send birthday cards, to feigning sexual pleasure so as not to upset a partner.

Feminist theorist Sara Ahmed argues that the Western obsession with acquiring and maintaining happiness is problematic as it's based on a normative life that isn't available to all (marrying, buying a house, having kids, etc.) Feminists are often stereotyped as being "killjoys" for questioning such norms, and could usefully reclaim this. Killing joy is a sensible reaction to the injustices of the world.

EXCLUSIONARY FEMINISMS

Exclusionary feminisms are reactions to more inclusive, intersectional third/fourth-wave approaches to gender inequality. They often attempt to limit who has access to the category of womanhood (such as excluding trans women), and to maintain a clear gender binary. They also regard certain groups as lacking agency, suggesting that they behave in the ways they do due to patriarchal oppression (such as trans men and sex workers).

ANTI SEX-WORK FEMINISTS IMAGINE THAT CRIMINALIZING SEX WORK WILL UNDERMINE CAPITALIST PATRIARCHY, BUT SEX WORK IN ITS CURRENT FORM IS JUST ONE RESULT OF THE CAPITALIST PATRIARCHY – ALONG WITH MANY OTHER OFTEN-EXPLOITATIVE FORMS OF WORK AND SEX.

– JUNO MAC & MOLLY SMITH authors of REVOLTING PROSTITUTES

EXPLOITATION OF MIGRANT WORKERS

TRAFFICKED DOMESTIC WORKERS

HATE CRIMES AGAINST TRANS WOMEN OF COLOUR

CURRENT FORMS OF SEX WORK

WOMEN'S UNPAID LABOUR IN THE HOME

TRANS

SEX WORK

IMPERIALISM

CAPITALISM

WHITE SUPREMACY

PATRIARCHY

Psychologist Bridgette Rickett points out that sensationalist media encourages "feminist infighting", and often presents it as a working-class vs. middle-class feminist fight. This leaves the wider systems and structures of oppression which adversely impact all of those involved unchallenged.

FEMININITIES FOR ALL GENDERS

Because gender is something we all draw upon from the world around us, it's not just women who draw upon – and develop – femininities (just as it's not just men who engage with masculinities).

However, due to the patriarchal understanding of man as norm and woman as other, the wider world often struggles to comprehend anyone drawing on femininities who is not regarded as a woman. Such expression is often heavily policed. Whereas anyone drawing on masculinities is understandable: of course people would want to be masculine.

That said, women who engage with supposedly masculine pursuits – like sports – often have to work hard to "compensate" by "proving" their femininity, and are portrayed in ways that emphasize this.

Gender scholar Adrian Yip points out how images and headlines about tennis star Serena Williams generally emphasize her feminine appearance or roles and criticize her aggression, while those of her male counterpart Novak Djokovic never have to downplay his "masculine" ambition or strength.

MALE FEMININITIES

Because masculinity is regarded as superior to femininity, anything associated with femininity on a man is highly visible, whereas masculinity on women is often unremarked.

For these reasons, male femininity remains hard to navigate. Boys who express any kind of femininity are still frequently bullied for being sissy or are assumed to be gay. Boys and men who are attracted to men – or who are feminine in any way – are therefore confronted with the double discrimination of homophobia and femmephobia.

CULTURAL STUDIES PROFESSOR STEPHEN MADDISON

WHILE "EFFEMINACY" AND "CAMPNESS" ARE OFTEN REJECTED OR RIDICULED, BOTH CROSS-GENDER IDENTIFICATION AND RELATIONSHIPS WITH WOMEN HAVE BEEN VITAL TO GAY MALE CULTURE.

AFTER YOU, M'AM

FEMME

"Femme" (or "fem") is a term from lesbian communities – now used across sexual and gender identities – to highlight the similar experiences of those embracing certain kinds of femininity. It's often a conscious expression of femininity, used by those in queer communities to point out how all gender is socially constructed.

There are many different kinds of femme identity and expression, such as hard femme for someone with feminine appearance and a dominant character, and stemme for someone who combines stud/butch and femme traits.

FEMMES EMPHASIZE GENDER AS POLITICAL IN INTENTIONALLY EMBRACING GENDERED EXPRESSIONS WHICH ARE REGARDED AS LESSER THAN MASCULINITY IN WIDER CULTURE. THEY MAY ALSO BE DELIBERATELY CELEBRATING BEAUTY PRACTICES WHICH ARE IMPORTANT IN THEIR RACE/CLASS CONTEXT BUT DENIGRATED BY WHITE, MIDDLE-CLASS PEOPLE.

GENDER SCHOLAR CAROLINE WALTERS

Terms such as "femmephobia", "trans-misogyny", "sissyphobia", and "misogynoir" reference specific groups' experiences of feminine devaluation. Femme can be erased or marginalized in queer cultures due to masculine ideals or a sense of butchness/trans masculinity as a more visible form of queerness.

EXPANDING AND CONTRACTING FEMININITIES

Many activists and academics are working to encourage girls – and people of other genders – to think critically about gender and to expand the forms of femininities available to them.

Emma Renold and Jessica Ringrose engage young people in art activism which enables them to share everyday experiences of gender norms and sexism, to find more empowered femininities through solidarity, and to shift school cultures.

For example, girls made a skirt comprised of rulers to draw attention to the everyday sexual harassment of boys using rulers to look up girls' skirts, and how school policies around skirt length implicitly blame girls rather than those who engage in non-consensual behaviour and the school culture itself.

JESSICA RINGROSE

EMMA RENOLD

With each new wave of feminism there is a risk of forgetting history, continually returning to old arguments, and dismissing previous vital ideas or practices. Such intergenerational activism enables younger people to learn from – and in return educate – feminists who developed their feminisms and femininities during earlier waves.

CHAPTER FIVE: NON-BINARY GENDERS

We've seen how both masculinity and femininity have been culturally defined in opposition to each other; how women have been regarded as "other" to men; and how most forms of masculinity are invested in avoiding being seen as in any way feminine.

Despite the diversity of masculinities and femininities, and the ways people of all genders can draw on these, gender is still seen as a binary in Western culture: there are men (who are masculine) and women (who are feminine). The recent non-binary movement – and its historical predecessors – questions this whole notion.

In this chapter we'll explore the gender binary more before asking what we can all learn from non-binary experience.

MANY PEOPLE THINK THERE'S THIS IMMOVABLE DIVIDE BETWEEN GENDERS, BUT FOR A LOT OF US, THAT ISN'T THE CASE.

BINARIES ON TOP OF BINARIES

Across time and space the gender binary has mapped onto other binaries which layer on top of it – often strengthening it. For example:

Women are located in the private sphere of home and family, men in the public sphere of work and politics, meaning that political systems benefit men more.

WOMEN ♀ | MEN ♂

INNER WORLD | OUTER WOR[L]

PRIVATE | PUBLIC

NATURE | CULTURE

Women are associated with nature, disorder, and emotions, men with culture, order, and rationality (although intersections with race and class position some men closer to women on these dimensions and some women as closer to men).

DISORDER | ORDER

EMOTION | REASON

IMPURE | PURE

BODY | MIND

NURTURING MOTHER | DOMINANT LEADER FATHER

Women are often seen as at more risk of impurity than men, and are associated more with their bodies. This means they have to prove their sexual purity and beauty to remain in the category of womanhood. Men are more associated with their minds and intelligence. There are similar binaries in play with motherhood and fatherhood, "maternal" meaning nurturing and caring and "paternal" exercising power and authority.

IMPLICATIONS OF BINARIES

All these binaries are flipped in some places and times, demonstrating that none are "natural" or universal divisions. Whichever way around they are though, binaries rarely benefit women. For example, when women are in the public domain it is often to enable scholarly, creative, or spiritual men to do their – more highly valued – work in private. When women are seen as closer to culture than nature they're often also responsible for taming men's "natural urges" and blamed if they don't.

This kind of binary underlies the rape culture that #MeToo highlighted. Rape culture refers to cultural attitudes around gender and sexuality that normalize non-consensual sex, for example seeing men as naturally active, unruly, dominant, and desiring; women as passive, taming, submissive, and desirable.

QUESTIONING THE BINARY

A good way to challenge the gender binary is to make a list of what's regarded as masculine and feminine in your time and place. Think about:

- **MESSAGES** YOU'VE RECEIVED ABOUT WHAT IT IS TO BE A *"real"* **MAN** OR **WOMAN**
- *Representations* OF **MEN** AND **WOMEN** IN **ADVERTISEMENTS**, TV SHOWS, MUSIC VIDEOS AND *MOVIES*
- THE WAYS PEOPLE TALK ABOUT **MEN** AND **WOMEN** IN *everyday conversations*

For each "feminine" trait include the "masculine" opposite, and vice versa. Once you have a list of opposites you can draw a spectrum between each of them and mark where you would be on that spectrum – if anywhere.

You could also ask yourself whether people you know fit perfectly into either side, and whether you can think of men who fit better on the feminine side and women who fit better on the masculine side (whether acquaintances, celebrities, or fictional characters).

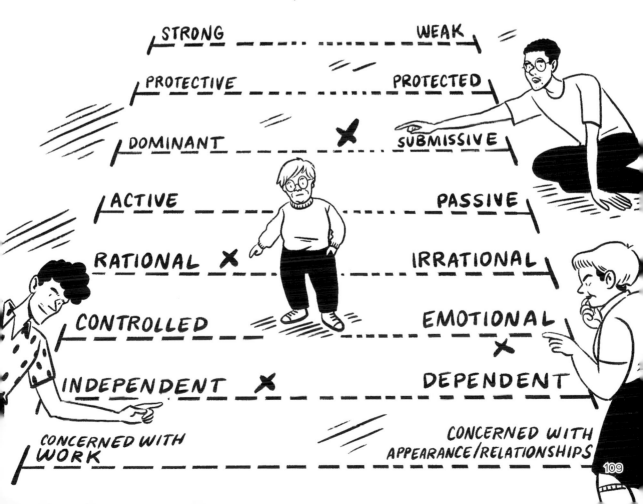

STRONG — WEAK
PROTECTIVE — PROTECTED
DOMINANT ✗ SUBMISSIVE
ACTIVE — PASSIVE
RATIONAL ✗ IRRATIONAL
CONTROLLED — EMOTIONAL ✗
INDEPENDENT ✗ DEPENDENT
CONCERNED WITH WORK — CONCERNED WITH APPEARANCE/RELATIONSHIPS

WHAT DO WE EVEN MEAN BY GENDER?

When we recognize that masculinity and femininity generally mean a whole range of things, not just one thing, we can see that many people are in different places on different spectrums. They contain a mix of what are regarded as more "masculine" and more "feminine" traits.

Identities and expressions that we considered earlier, like "hard femme" or "tender masculinity" also call into question the gender binary. Where would we locate these in relation to masculinity or femininity?

When you break it down like this it becomes clear that gender isn't a simple binary but many complex overlapping spectrums which we may move around on over time, and which intersect profoundly with other aspects of our identities and experiences such as race, class, age, sexuality, and disability. We all have a unique relationship to gender.

WHY ARE WE SO INTO THE GENDER BINARY?

Given that gender isn't a simple either/or, why are we so wedded to the binary? Why do we find any challenges so threatening? Well, we're taught throughout life that there is great pleasure in the binary: fitting well into masculinity/femininity is a way to belong and gain acceptance. It is also presented as the passport to love and great sex – founded on the idea of opposite, complementary genders.

There's big money in it – gendering products means more income. And self-help can sell simple solutions to complex problems if we buy into the gender binary.

If we have taught the gender binary to others ourselves, we may not want to confront the damage it has caused. If the binary has been bad for us, we may not want to know that things could have been otherwise if we hadn't struggled so hard to conform to it.

GENDER COMPLEMENTARITY, HETERONORMATIVITY, AND ROMANTIC LOVE

As we saw on page 14, binary gender is also bound up with heteronormativity: the cultural assumption that heterosexuality is the normal, natural, or best way to be, and that men and women are therefore complementary and fit together physically and psychologically.

Heteronormativity informs so much of our treasured literary and popular culture. The "romantic" ideal of two opposite, complementary genders is seen again and again, from fairy tales to Hollywood romcoms. However, this ideal is bad for women, for men, and for relationships between them.

For example, existential philosopher Simone de Beauvoir argued that treating women as unequal denies men the opportunity of sharing their lives with a mutually supportive partner. Meanwhile women are sold the idea that relationships are the big adventure of their lives and that their only source of pleasure is in making themselves a desirable object.

In her book *All About Love*, bell hooks explores how gender complementarity is taught to children, and how the outcome denies them the possibility of real love. She says that boys are silenced by the patriarchal world that doesn't want them to claim their true feelings. Girls are taught that they must become something other than themselves in order to attract and please others. Women and men are therefore both encouraged to present a false self in order to control and/or please each other. Secrets and lies erode trust and the ability to form a genuine, loving connection.

Actor Terry Crews links this to more obviously toxic forms of entitlement and abuse in his famous #MeToo quote:

NON-BINARY GENDER

It's politically important to challenge the gender binary so as to free people from restrictions and from unequal treatment on the basis of gender. It's also important in relation to recognizing those who aren't men or women.

"Non-binary" ("NB" or "enby") is the most common umbrella term for people who experience their gender as neither male nor female. A diverse range of experiences fit under this umbrella.

THE EXTENT OF NON-BINARY EXPERIENCE

It's hard to estimate the extent of non-binary gender because few national surveys offer options beyond "male" and "female". Also, until the recent non-binary movement, very few people identified in non-binary ways even if this was their experience. This is reflected in the different numbers you get when you measure non-binary identity or experience.

In 2014, before there was much non-binary recognition, activist Nat Titman found that around one in 250 people identified themselves as other than male or female when given the option to do so. However, in the same year psychologist Daphna Joel found that when people were asked whether they experience themselves as to some extent the "other" gender, "both genders" and/or "neither gender", over a third said that they did.

As non-binary people become more visible in popular culture, it's likely that larger numbers of people will identify in this way. For example, over 7,000 NB people responded to the 2018 UK government national LGBT survey – more than trans men and women put together.

THE NON-BINARY MOVEMENT

As we saw in Chapter 1, many places have non-binary understandings of gender, and there are many historical precedents for non-binary people, so non-binary gender is nothing new.

Current non-binary movements also have historical precedents in older feminist, queer, and trans movements.

NOTIONS OF FEMININITY AND MASCULINITY ARE COLONIAL CONSTRUCTS THAT HAVE FREQUENTLY PUSHED MORE COMPLEX NOTIONS OF GENDER AND SEXUALITY INTO A BINARY.

CULTURAL STUDIES PROFESSOR FREYA SCHIWY

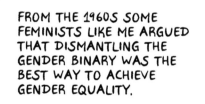

FROM THE 1960S SOME FEMINISTS LIKE ME ARGUED THAT DISMANTLING THE GENDER BINARY WAS THE BEST WAY TO ACHIEVE GENDER EQUALITY.

PSYCHOLOGIST SANDRA BEM

Since the 1980s queer activism and queer theory have critiqued normative binary assumptions of both gender (male/female) and sexuality (straight/gay) as key roots of oppression. We discussed this in our book *Queer: A Graphic History.*

Since the 1990s, trans activism and trans studies have also challenged binary gender assumptions. We'll say more about trans activism and trans studies in Chapter 6.

GENDER REVOLUTION!

Recently various shifts have set the scene for a more visible and vocal non-binary movement:

- **2011**: WORLD PROFESSIONAL ASSOCIATION FOR TRANSGENDER HEALTH UPDATES ITS STANDARDS OF CARE TO BE MORE INCLUSIVE OF NON-BINARY GENDERS

- **2014**: Facebook's "gender revolution" offers over 50 possible gender identity categories for users, as well as a gender neutral "they" pronoun option

- **2016**: A non-binary actor plays a non-binary character on a mainstream American TV show, **ASIA KATE DILLON** in **BILLIONS**

- **2013**: the American Psychiatric Association's Diagnostic and Statistical Manual (DSM-5) shifts its classification to one which is more inclusive of NON-BINARY PEOPLE

- **2014**: BEYOND THE BINARY ONLINE MAGAZINE LAUNCHES, AIMING TO RE-BALANCE THE INVISIBILITY OF NON-BINARY GENDERS AND GIVE NON-BINARY PEOPLE A PLATFORM

I DID A BIT OF RESEARCH AND DISCOVERED THAT FEMALE IS AN ASSIGNED SEX AND NON-BINARY IS IN REFERENCE TO GENDER IDENTITY AND THOSE ARE TWO DIFFERENT THINGS. IT FINALLY HELPED ME PUT LANGUAGE TO A FEELING THAT I'D HAD MY ENTIRE LIFE ... SOMETIMES YOU HAVE TO SEE THE THING TO KNOW THAT IT EXISTS.

- **2018**: URUGUAY BECOMES THE LATEST COUNTRY TO ENABLE PEOPLE TO SELF-DETERMINE THEIR GENDER/SEX INCLUDING OTHER DESCRIPTIONS THAN MALE/FEMALE OR MAN/WOMAN

WHAT DO NON-BINARY PEOPLE WANT?

A major issue for non-binary people is lack of visibility in society and the media. Every day, in multiple ways, people are categorized as male or female and are subject to assumptions that these are the only possible categories. Such misgendering wears people down as they have to choose either to continually out themselves – facing anything from repeated questioning to discrimination and hate crime – or to remain closeted and deal with the stress of keeping a key part of themselves hidden.

Along with legal recognition, protections, and inclusive services, cultural shifts in language are important for non-binary inclusion. For example, using:

- **MX** TITLE OPTIONS AS WELL AS MR/MS

- SINGULAR **THEY** PRONOUNS AS WELL AS **HE/SHE**

PERFECTLY GRAMMATICALLY CORRECT!

LINGUIST TOM SCOTT

- "FOLKS" OR "PEOPLE" RATHER THAN "GUYS" OR "LADIES"

- "FRIENDS AND COLLEAGUES" RATHER THAN "LADIES AND GENTLEMEN"

#ThisIsWhatNonBinaryLooksLike

As with so many other movements, there is a risk that the non-binary movement only challenges the gender binary but leaves other aspects of imperialist, white supremacist, capitalist patriarchy unquestioned, or even perpetuates other oppressions.

This can be seen in the way that images we do see of non-binary people tend to be young, white, slim, non-disabled, wearing "fashionable" clothes, and either obviously androgynous or masculine-of-centre.

Non-binary activists Fox Fisher and Owl (Ugla Stefanía) started the hashtag #ThisIsWhatNonBinaryLooksLike to capture more diversity of non-binary people.

SOCIAL MEDIA INCREASES OUR ENGAGEMENT WITH MORE DIVERSE PEOPLE THAN WE FIND IN OUR IMMEDIATE OFFLINE COMMUNITIES. THAT CAN MAKE THINGS BETTER FOR EVERYONE.

ALOK VAID-MENON

AARON PHILIP

119

NON-BINARY AS IN BETWEEN OR BOTH

For the rest of this chapter we'll explore various non-binary identities and experiences and what they may have to offer to everybody, including those who identify as women or men.

NB understandings

Some non-binary people experience themselves as somewhere in between masculinity and femininity, or as incorporating elements of both. For example, futch and butchfemme people incorporate elements of both gender expressions.

How this may be useful for everyone

This allows us to view gender as a spectrum – or multiple spectrums – rather than two boxes, which opens up the possibility that we might incorporate aspects seen as "masculine" and "feminine" into how we present ourselves or act.

This type of NB expression does retain the idea that there are coherent binary masculine and feminine positions we can locate ourselves in relation to. However, it breaks the direct correlation between these and a male/female assigned sex.

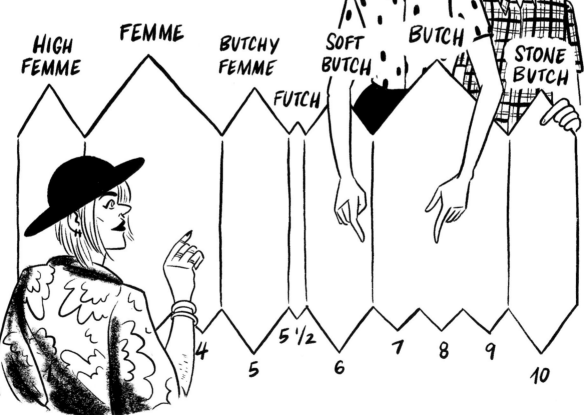

HIGH FEMME FEMME BUTCHY FEMME FUTCH SOFT BUTCH BUTCH STONE BUTCH

4   5   5½   6   7   8   9   10

NON-BINARY AS NEITHER OR BEYOND

NB understandings

Some non-binary people experience themselves as having no gender. Others experience themselves as a further gender beyond man or woman.

How this may be useful for everyone

Just as people on the asexual and aromantic spectrum have taught us that we don't all experience sexual or romantic attraction, people on the agender spectrum teach us that it's completely legitimate to have no gender, or a muted sense of gender.

Non-gendered people like Christie Elan-Cane and Norrie May-Welby have been at the forefront of campaigning for gender X options on documents like passports, which could increase cultural awareness – and legitimacy – of gender diversity.

ACTIVISTS LIKE THIS REMIND US THAT THE PERSONAL IS POLITICAL FOR ALL OF US: HOWEVER WE EXPERIENCE, EXPRESS, AND IDENTIFY OUR GENDERS, WE'RE CONTRIBUTING TO GENDER CULTURE.

NON-BINARY AS FLUID

NB understandings

Genderfluid people experience their gender as shifting over time, whether over years, months, or the course of the day. They may express their gender differently and/or identify using different names or pronouns at different times. We might see Doctor Who's regenerations as a nice way of representing this.

How this may be useful for everyone

Considering gender as fluid can be liberating. Think about how you experienced, expressed, and identified your gender as a child, a teenager, and an adult at different ages. What words did you use and have used about you, and how well did they fit? How did you visibly express your gender? How did you experience it?

Many cultures have a sense of gender shifting over a lifetime. For example, male children and very old people are associated with femininity, as in "women and children first" and older people being regarded as dependent. Postmenopausal women are sometimes seen as losing their femininity or as more work-focused. These cultural perceptions often weave into our sense of identity, as we saw in Chapter 2.

RIGHT NOW, I'M A STRANGER TO MYSELF. THERE'S ECHOES OF WHO I WAS, AND A SORT OF CALL TOWARDS WHO I AM, AND I HAVE TO HOLD MY NERVE AND TRUST ALL THESE NEW INSTINCTS, SHAPE MYSELF TOWARDS THEM. I'LL BE FINE, IN THE END.

NON-BINARY AS PLURAL

NB understandings

Related to gender fluidity is the concept of gender plurality. Bigender, pangender, and polygender people experience themselves as having more than one gender at the same time, or as shifting between them over time. This can be like having two or more alter-egos or personas with different gender identities and expressions, or it can involve experiencing oneself as more masculine, feminine, or androgynous at different times, for example.

How this may be useful for everyone

Many therapists and authors have argued that we're actually all plural selves rather than a singular "me". Some selves are disowned over time – often those deemed culturally inappropriate for our assumed gender – while other selves are foregrounded.

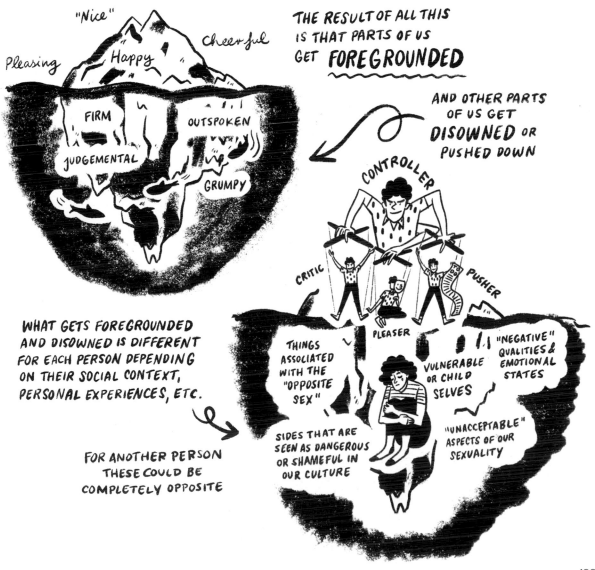

BREAKING THE BINARY FOR EVERYONE

One backlash against non-binary people is the accusation that they want to end gender. While this certainly isn't everyone's agenda, many trans and NB activists would like to see a shift in how the world sees gender because the binary, static way of understanding gender is bad for everybody. As we've seen, that might involve understanding gender as more diverse, fluid, and plural.

In the previous two chapters we saw how different attributes are culturally labelled masculine and feminine and how a major part of doing masculinity or femininity is denying or disowning the "other" attributes in ourselves.

GENDER IDENTIFICATION IS A KIND OF MELANCHOLIA. WE ALL LEARN THAT BEING ONE GENDER IS PROHIBITED TO US AND WE INTERNALIZE THAT PROHIBITION, BUT FEEL IT AS AN UNEXPLAINED SENSE OF LOSS OR SADNESS.

GENDER THEORIST JUDITH BUTLER

Even though all gender expressions and experiences are technically available to all of us, it's very hard to do genders other than the ones deemed culturally acceptable for our bodies.

NON-BINARY AND TRANS

"Trans" is an umbrella term for anybody who hasn't remained in the sex/gender they were assumed to be at birth. Babies are almost exclusively assumed to be either male or female at birth. Therefore, like trans men and trans women, non-binary people don't identify with their birth-assigned sex/gender.

INSTEAD OF TALKING ABOUT "TRANS AND NON-BINARY PEOPLE" IT'S BETTER TO TALK ABOUT "TRANS PEOPLE INCLUDING NON-BINARY PEOPLE".

AUTHOR & SINGER-SONGWRITER
CN LESTER

However not all non-binary people identify as trans. Some associate "trans" with social or medical transitions which they don't necessarily seek. Like trans women and men, some non-binary people seek gender-affirming hormones and/or surgeries, and some do not.

Some people use the words "queer" or "trans" instead of "non-binary" to describe themselves, so as not to define themselves in relation to the binary. In the next chapter we'll explore more the meanings of trans, and the trans/cis binary.

CHAPTER SIX: TRANS & CIS

Trans – or transgender – is a big umbrella that covers many, many different experiences.

Trans means "across from" and cis means "on the side of". So cis – or cisgender – people are those who remain in the the gender they were assumed to be at birth. Trans/cis is another binary we can usefully question given the massive diversity of experiences under trans and cis, and the overlaps between them.

TO ME, BEING TRANS MEANS MY BODY IS GENDER NON-CONFORMING AND MY GENDER EXPRESSION IS FLUID AND MY GENDER IDENTITY IS REALLY PERSONAL.

SABAH CHOUDREY

I ALWAYS THOUGHT OF MYSELF AS A GIRL WHO WAS CURSED BY BIOLOGY.

JANET MOCK

I IDENTIFIED AS BUTCH, THEN NON-BINARY, NOW AS A TRANS MAN.

S. BEAR BERGMAN

I REMEMBER WHEN I WAS 10 REALIZING WITH GREAT DISAPPOINTMENT THAT I WASN'T GOING TO MAGICALLY TURN INTO A GIRL I ASSUMED I MUST BE A GAY MAN FOR MANY YEARS.

JUNO DAWSON

I ALWAYS KNEW I WASN'T A MAN, BUT AFTER I TRANSITIONED I REALIZED I WASN'T A WOMAN EITHER.

KATE BORNSTEIN

IT'S A BIG ENOUGH UMBRELLA

So trans people may:

- Experience their gender as static and fixed, or as fluid and changing over time.
- Identify with a binary or non-binary gender.
- Go through social transitions – like changing their name, pronoun, or gender expression – or not.
- Go through medical transitions relating to their gender – like taking hormones or having surgeries – or not.
- Be out about being trans, or not.
- Experience gender dysphoria (feeling strange or negative about their body and/or gender), or gender euphoria, or anything in between.

If you think about it, all of these can also apply to cis people. For example:

TREATING TRANS

THE HISTORY OF TRANS IS ROOTED IN THE SCIENTIFIC ATTEMPT TO CATEGORIZE "DEVIANT" FORMS OF SEXUALITY AND GENDER EXPRESSION IN THE LATE 19TH CENTURY. BY THE MID 20TH CENTURY SEXOLOGISTS LIKE HARRY BENJAMIN AND JOHN MONEY TURNED THEIR ATTENTION TO TRANS PEOPLE.

HOSPITAL FOR THE INSANE

HEAD OF GENDERED INTELLIGENCE,
JAY STEWART

Benjamin popularized the term "transsexual" and saw it as a medical condition which could be treated with "sex change" operations. Following this, many medics saw transsexualism as a form of intersex: caused by a physiological difference between trans and cis people from birth. This is where the common narrative of trans people being "born in the wrong body" came from.

However others – like Money – argued that gender was socially imposed – and could therefore be inconsistent with a person's physiology (hormones, chromosomes, sex characteristics, etc.). He suggested that a child could be raised any gender.

ECHOES OF THE PAST

These arguments echo through modern debates about whether being trans is socially or biologically rooted. On both sides some people use these arguments to justify trans people's existence, and some to critique it. Both sides are questionable because - as we saw in Chapter 2 - gender is a complex interweaving of our biology, psychological experiences, and social world.

Just because something can be found in the brain doesn't mean people were "born that way", because our experiences also alter our brain. There's also a dangerous tendency to slide from "it's biological" to deciding to test people to "see if they're really trans".

Increasing numbers of trans people over time doesn't mean its cause is social. As writer Julia Serano points out, the number of left-handed people has increased recently because they're no longer forced to write with their right hand.

Whatever the extent of biological, social, or other reasons for an individual's transness - or cisness - it should make no difference to their right to be treated decently and to access services to help them have a comfortable relationship with their gender and body.

TRANSGENDER STUDIES

The activist-academic area of transgender studies emerged in the 1990s in response to the prevailing culture: the medicalization of trans experience as a disorder, and anti-trans feminism which didn't see trans women as women. Trans studies scholars continue to research the lived experience of trans people, producing gender theories that include trans, and challenging clinics, laws, and education to become more inclusive.

Sandy Stone's *The Empire Strikes Back: A Posttranssexual Manifesto* was a response to Janice Raymond's anti-trans book *The Transsexual Empire*. Stone argues that trans experiences are complex and resistant to singular explanations and simplifications that many feminists, medics, and researchers hold.

Leslie Feinberg's "Transgender Liberation" pamphlet helped popularize the term "transgender". It encompasses more diversity than "transsexual", which was a psychiatric diagnosis often assumed to necessitate a medical transition. "Transgender" (and its abbreviation, trans) also includes those who don't undergo surgeries and/or hormones due to choice or lack of access.

MARSHA P. JOHNSON

MISS MAJOR

SANDY STONE

POWER TO THE PEOPLE

ANGELA K. DOUGLAS

SYLVIA RIVERA

Trans people campaigned way before the 1990s though: they were central to key LGBT rights moments, such as Stonewall in New York, Compton's Cafeteria in San Francisco, and the first Pride march.

THE TRANS MOVEMENT

The trans movement has existed for decades and has faced many challenges.

In Britain in the 1990s, Christine Burns and Stephen Whittle set up Press for Change, which fought to get trans people legally recognized in their genders.

In 2014 in the US, Susan Striker and Paisley Currah established the first non-medical journal on trans, *TSQ: Transgender Studies Quarterly.*

These examples finally put trans people themselves at the heart of both the legal process about them and the academic study of their lives.

Memoirs, autobiographies, and other personal narratives have been a key part of the trans movement from the start. These can help people to make sense of their own lives and to claim back trans knowledge and expertise for trans people.

PFC CAMPAIGNERS ↗

HOWEVER, MEMOIRS CAN SUGGEST A SINGULAR TRANS NARRATIVE, OR THAT TRANS PEOPLE SHOULD EXPLAIN THEMSELVES IN WAYS CIS PEOPLE DON'T HAVE TO. THAT'S WHY I TRIED TO RE-IMAGINE THE TRANS MEMOIR.

JULIET JACQUES

TRANS NARRATIVES

In CN Lester's memoir *Trans Like Me*, they point out that many cis people only know of trans lives from media representations, which are often dehumanizing, inaccurate, and present trans people as only victims or villains. This is particularly concerning when cis people make many decisions that impact trans lives - as parents, practitioners, or policy-makers.

TV shows and movies often "reveal" trans characters' status for humour or dramatic purposes, and it's generally presented as the only - or most important - thing about them. Rounded characters who happen to be trans are still rare.

Since 2013, popular shows like *Transparent, Orange is the New Black, Sense8* and *Grey's Anatomy* finally featured trans actors playing trans characters that moved away from old stereotypes.

CENTRING TRANS VOICES

For decades the main voices about trans experience have been those of cis people – whether questioning and threatening trans existence, or acting as "saviours" of trans people, often according to a narrative which depicts trans people as victims or broken and in need of fixing. Documentaries, reality TV, and talk shows have focused on specific trans stories, particularly binary before/after stories of medical transition. This reduces trans experience to a simple singular narrative, and reduces trans bodies to genitals.

Increasingly, trans people are creating art, performances, writing, and media about their lives, which leads to a greater sense of the diversity of trans experience, and aspects of trans lives beyond being trans.

THE TRANSGENDER TIPPING POINT

The year 2014 was hailed "the transgender tipping point" due to increasing trans visibility and decreasing stigma across a range of institutions.

The year previously, the American Psychiatric Association changed their category of "Gender Identity Disorder" to "Gender Dysphoria". This removed much of the stigma because trans people were no longer seen as *being disordered* (or mentally ill), but rather as *experiencing discomfort* with their gender. This improved the treatment trans people received from health professionals. Along with more trans programming on mainstream TV, Laverne Cox made the cover of *Time* magazine, and Janet Mock's memoir *Redefining Realness* became a bestseller. The first trans pride march in Europe took place.

The tipping point led to increased interest in – and awareness of – trans and trans rights. Subsequently, Caitlin Jenner made the cover of *Vanity Fair*, many countries granted trans people equal rights, including the right to self-define their gender, and many banned conversion therapies that attempt to stop somebody from being trans.

THE TRANS MORAL PANIC

The tipping point represented progress, but it came with a cultural backlash. By 2017 this tipped all the way into moral panic.

A documentary about trans and gender questioning kids in Canada kicked off public debates. Legal tussles over transgender bathroom rights in the US prompted anxious stereotyping of trans people as perpetrators of violence (although they're far more commonly victims of it). Donald Trump attempted to ban trans people from serving in the US military (an order blocked by the courts but which was raised again in 2018). In the UK, there was furore over trans women's identities, gender-neutral children's clothing, the existence of non-binary people, and more.

The media frequently set up debates between trans people and those who dispute their existence, presenting transphobia as a legitimate "side".

TRANS AND INTERSEX

Why the trans moral panic? There are likely many reasons, but different responses to trans and intersex people provide some answers. Remember from Chapter 2 that intersex people are those whose anatomy or physiology differs from contemporary ideas of what constitute typical male and female.

Intersex activist Susannah Temko points out that many intersex people undergo operations as babies that are medically unnecessary and lead to adverse effects in later life, such as the impairment of sexual sensation and the impact of such early trauma often having been kept secret. However, we very rarely hear about intersex surgeries in the press, while there is an obsession with trans bodies and surgeries.

Intersex surgeries bring people's bodies in line with gender norms, while trans people are seen as threatening them. This suggests the panic is really about gender norms.

THE MEDIA AREN'T WORRIED ABOUT INTERSEX SURGERIES ON BABIES, BUT THEY'RE HUGELY CONCERNED ABOUT TREATING TRANS KIDS — DESPITE THE FACT THAT THEY RARELY UNDERGO SURGERY OR HORMONAL TREATMENTS TILL THEY'RE ADULTS.

TRANS CAMPAIGNER & JOURNALIST PARIS LEES

NEWS MEDIA ARE OBSESSED WITH TRANS PEOPLE, BUT RARELY COVER THE ALARMING RATES OF TRANSPHOBIC BULLYING IN SCHOOLS, OR HOW NEARLY HALF OF TRANS KIDS HAVE ATTEMPTED SUICIDE. THIS GULF IN REPORTING SPEAKS VOLUMES.

INTERSECTING TRANS

It's vital to consider intersectionality when it comes to trans experience. The dead remembered on Trans Day of Remembrance are almost all trans women and trans feminine people of colour, many of whom are also working class and work as sex workers.

CeCe McDonald is a trans woman of colour who defended herself against a violent attack in 2011. Her conviction and incarceration highlighted the way race and trans status intersect to determine which lives matter in the US.

THE REALITY OF TRANS PEOPLE'S LIVES IS THAT SO OFTEN WE ARE TARGETS OF VIOLENCE. WE EXPERIENCE DISCRIMINATION DISPROPORTIONATELY TO THE REST OF THE COMMUNITY. OUR UNEMPLOYMENT RATE IS TWICE THE NATIONAL AVERAGE; IF YOU ARE A TRANS PERSON OF COLOUR, THAT RATE IS FOUR TIMES THE NATIONAL AVERAGE.

FREE CeCe!

Laverne Cox presents a documentary on one of the most controversial imprisonments of a trans woman in America

ACTRESS & CAMPAIGNER LAVERNE COX

As psychologist Stephanie Davis points out, Queer and Trans People of Colour (QTPOC) experience gender very differently to white people. For example, trans masculine Black and Asian people know they risk being treated as potentially violent or terrorists if they express their masculinity.

Neither trans nor disabled people are given ownership of their bodies. Medical models portray both trans and disabled people as in need of curing, fixing, and reaching an abled/ cis status. To get assistance, disabled trans people often have to downplay either their transness or their disability.

TRANS RIGHT VERSUS OTHER RIGHTS?

News media - with its focus on binary debate - often presents trans rights as in opposition to lesbian and gay rights, and trans feminism in opposition to feminism as a whole. For example, the potential for medical transition is presented as a pressure on kids against remaining as a gender non-conforming person. This idea that you can either be trans or lesbian/gay, trans or feminist, trans or gender non-conforming fails to acknowledge the many LGB, feminist, and queer trans people.

After anti-trans feminists protested trans inclusion in London Pride in 2018, many LGB people and feminists came out in support of trans people.

SOJOURNER TRUTH SAID WHAT SHE SAID BECAUSE BLACK WOMEN WERE DENIED THE CATEGORY OF WOMANHOOD. IF MY LIBERATION COMES WITHOUT THE LIBERATION OF TRANS WOMEN THEN MY LIBERATION IS MEANINGLESS.

MARAI LARASI
EXECUTIVE DIRECTOR OF **IMKAAN** - AN ORGANIZATION WHICH WORKS TO PREVENT VIOLENCE AGAINST MARGINALIZED WOMEN AND GIRLS

CISNESS, CISNORMATIVITY, AND CISCOURSES

We've seen that being cisgender means remaining in the gender you were assumed to be at birth.

As with masculinity, heterosexuality, and whiteness, cisness has often been assumed to be the superior way of being, and therefore as not requiring scrutiny or study.

Ben Vincent writes about flipping the power dynamic in research and having trans scholars examine "ciscourses": things cis people say and do which perpetuate and reinforce cisnormativity.

QUESTIONING THE TRANS/CIS BINARY

Another good reason to study cisnormativity is that it's often bad for cis people. We've seen throughout this book how holding rigidly to gender norms can result in toxic forms of masculinity or femininity, which are bad for men and women, for their relationships, and for everybody else – for example in the rates of suicide and criminal convictions in men, or depression and body-image issues in women.

Author and therapist Alex Iantaffi suggests that one way to loosen the tight grip on gender norms is to question the trans/cis binary. To what extent does anybody stay in the sex/gender they were assumed to be at birth? Do we not all experience shifts in gender identity, experience, and expression to some degree over the course of our lives?

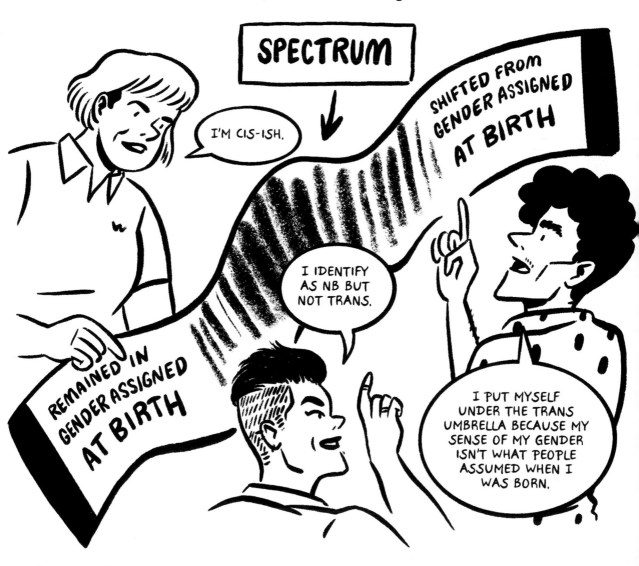

Some people who experience themselves as gender diverse but don't identify or express this in ways obvious to others recognize their cis privilege. They might use words like "cis-ish" or "cish" as well as non-binary terms to define themselves.

TRANS BODIES, TRANS SEX

Trans people's bodies and sexualities are often policed. They are expected to aspire to bodies – including genitals – that are as close as possible to cis bodies and capable of hetero sex. The psychiatric profession has questioned whether trans people are "really trans" if they find the idea of themselves as a gender different to that assumed at birth erotic. This is despite the fact that many cis people also find it erotic to express their femininity or masculinity.

I'M NOT A "GIRL IN A BOY'S BODY", I'M A GIRL. THIS IS MY BODY. GIRLS HAVE ALL KINDS OF BODIES.

SOPHIE LABELLE, CARTOONIST

ASSIGNED male COMICS

facebook.com/assignedmale
assignedmale.tumblr.com

I HAVEN'T FAILED TO "PASS" AS A WOMAN, I WANT TO LOOK TRANSGENDER. I DON'T NEED TO BE SEEN AS WOMAN, AS A TRANS WOMAN. I AM HAPPY TO BE SEEN AS A TRANS PERSON, BORN TRANS WITH A TRANS BODY CAPABLE OF FLUIDITY AND CHANGE.

AUTHOR OF QUEER SEX, JUNO ROCHE

ACTIVIST-ACADEMIC, H HOWITT

GIVEN THE LIMITATIONS PEOPLE PLACE AROUND SEX DUE TO ASSUMPTIONS ABOUT HOW GENITALS SHOULD WORK, AND WHAT THINGS DIFFERENT GENDERS SHOULD DO, TRANS SEX HAS MUCH TO TEACH EVERYONE ABOUT THE POSSIBILITIES AND POTENTIALS OF BODIES, PLEASURE, AND GENDER.

141

TRANS TIME

Trans scholars Kat Gupta and Ruth Pearce explore the concept of trans time, pointing out that the way trans people are treated often denies them vital experiences of time. For example, the way the media misgender trans people refuses them the possibility of a future in their gender. Meanwhile, popular trans narratives may mean they have to erase their pasts to be granted rights and recognition.

Policies and practices often expect trans people to be clairvoyant: promising to remain a certain way forever in order to access services or recognition. Lack of services means those seeking physical transition often feel their life is delayed while they wait for treatment.

But trans people also find ways to travel, trick, and transcend time, often experiencing non-linear life courses. They might go through more than one puberty, with the second occurring later in life. Many trans people look younger, and some talk of an age in "trans years": the number of years since they came out or transitioned, in addition to their number of years on the planet.

Many regenerate over time, as they find bodies, identities, and expressions that are a better fit. Some time-travel back to reclaim previous parts of themselves.

TRANS SPACE

Most trans people have negative experiences of space. They're unsafe in many public and domestic spaces, risking discrimination, ridicule, and even violent attack if their transness is read. At the same time, they're often seen as a danger in spaces like public toilets or changing rooms, and are called millennial "snowflakes" and dismissed if they campaign for spaces to be safer for trans people, for example by excluding transphobic voices or by ensuring people use correct pronouns.

Many also have the disorienting experience of moving through space and being read differently at different times: but in ways that rarely mirror the ways they experience themselves. The affirming experience most people take for granted of having themselves correctly reflected in the spaces they occupy day-to-day is unavailable.

Some trans people shapeshift in order to navigate space safely. On the street they may present as more feminine to avoid being perceived as a threat to others, or more masculine if they perceive a risk of harassment. They may learn in which spaces they are safe to present themselves authentically, and in which spaces they need to present partially or to pass as cis.

TRANS IN RELATIONSHIP

Transness – and cisness – can be seen as something that resides in relationships rather than in individuals. Our gender experiences emerge in specific family systems and community contexts. Systems and communities can operate in ways that enforce cisnormativity or invite gender diversity; ways which enable being out as trans or which limit possible gender expressions. Family and school community support is a major buffer against mental health struggles in young trans people.

Each person's gender experience and expression has the potential to shape these systems and networks also.

GENDER AWARENESS

RE-EVALUATION

Empathy

WHAT WOULD HAPPEN IF GENDER CREATIVITY WAS CELEBRATED, NOT PUNISHED? IF TRANS PEOPLE WERE SEEN AS A GIFT TO THOSE AROUND THEM, PROMPTING THEM TO REFLECT ON THEIR OWN GENDERS AND LIVES TOO?

ARTIST & PERFORMER
TRAVIS ALABANZA

LIBERATING GENDER FOR ALL

Instead of exploring and seeking to explain "difference", we would do well to ask what we can all learn from the margins: the people at the cutting edge of understanding and experiencing gender, sexuality, identity, bodies, relationships, etc.

It goes beyond gender. For example, by working to create a safe place for trans people to get their hair cut, Open Barbers developed practices which would be helpful for all hairdressers. Thinking about the gender dysphoria clients might experience led them to develop practices like a book of haircuts without faces for people to choose from, and checking in throughout the process as to how it feels. Considering how trans intersects with other aspects of identity and experience, they created a sliding pricing scale, where price is not attached to the gender of a client. Being a gender inclusive hairdressers in an inner city location also has the ripple effect of increasing gender awareness in the community.

GENDERED INTELLIGENCE

Perhaps we could all aspire to gendered intelligence: aiming for a world where people are no longer constrained by narrow perceptions and expectations of gender, and where diverse gender expressions are visible and valued. This might look like:

CHAPTER SEVEN: THE FUTURE OF GENDER

People have always looked back through time, and to other communities around the world, in the hope of finding utopias where gender is done better. We've seen the risks of doing this throughout the book. People easily read the past – and other cultures – through their own understandings, hopes, and fears. They appropriate things they don't really understand and/or put far too much pressure on certain groups to create a better world: often groups who've experienced the most oppression.

So what if we re-imagined gender-alternative or future realities rather than searching for this in the past or the present? As author of *The Psychology of Gender*, Gary W. Wood, points out, sci-fi, fantasy, and other forms of speculative fiction open up important spaces for imagining gender differently without placing these burdens on real people. There's even a literary award, the Tiptree, for works which encourage the exploration and expansion of gender.

FEMINISM, OF COURSE, HAS ALWAYS BEEN AN EXERCISE IN SCIENCE FICTION.

AUTHOR LAURIE PENNY

THE PAST

THE FUTURE

GENDER SWITCHING

Fiction explores gender most commonly with the gender switch, in which people pass as the "opposite" gender, or become a different gender some or all of the time. There are hundreds of books, TV shows, and films that use this trope, such as *The Hot Chick* or *It's a Boy Girl Thing*.

Another common trope is using a parallel universe in which gender roles are flipped. In one episode of the TV series *Red Dwarf*, the crew enter such a universe – a world where women have always had all the power – and encounter female versions of themselves. The humour centres around how disgusted the male characters are to be treated in the way in which they treat women.

One limitation of these genres is that they can reinforce the sense that gender involves binary opposites. Also gender switches can be read as sensationalizing, simplifying, and ridiculing the reality of trans experience.

MRS. DOUBTFIRE

APPLIED PHLEBUTINIUM ZAP!

TOOTSIE

RED DWARF

GENDER DYSTOPIAS

Gender dystopian fictions imagine a world in which gender dynamics are worse than – but echo – the current situation. For example in *The Stepford Wives* (novel 1972; films 1975, 2004) men turn women into docile servants: a metaphor for the ways in which women are expected to do unrewarded labour, and treated as objects that men are entitled to (see Chapter 4). The movie *Get Out* (2017) explores objectification in a similar way, dealing with how black bodies are treated as property by white people.

Perhaps the most popular recent example of this is *The Handmaid's Tale*, Margaret Atwood's 1985 novel, adapted for TV in 2017, and its 2019 sequel *The Testaments*. In a future, post-apocalyptic US, women have no rights and many are forced into sexual servitude as "handmaids". A powerful and chilling story, the reception of *The Handmaid's Tale* by white feminists has been critiqued for failing to recognize how closely it mirrors how black women actually *have* been treated.

GENDER UTOPIAS

Gender utopias imagine worlds with better gender systems or dynamics than our current one. Such utopias are often entirely female, or at least matriarchal. For example, *Herland* by Charlotte Perkins-Gillman imagines a hidden all-female society in which women live in harmony. *The Female Man* by Joanna Russ imagines alternate versions of the same person to juxtapose a dystopia where men and women are at war with an all-lesbian utopia of peaceful farming and advanced technology. *The Legend of Wonder Woman* by Renae De Liz is a recent feminist reimagining of Themyscira - an Amazonian utopia.

All these examples seem to assume that women-led societies would inevitably be more peaceful and cooperative. Similarly, *Sleeping Beauties* by Stephen and Owen King employs the "gendercide" trope where one gender is wiped out. Men descend into chaos while the sleeping women begin to form a utopian fantasy future.

As psychologist Lynne Segal argues, the feminist idea that only women - because of their superior humanity - can save the world from disaster is problematic because it's based on a mistaken belief in innate and essential differences between binary genders.

IS THE FUTURE FEMALE?

Some authors have explored whether things would really be better if women had the physical and/or cultural power men currently have.

GALADRIEL IN *LORD OF THE RINGS* BY JRR TOLKIEN

INSTEAD OF A DARK LORD, YOU WOULD HAVE A QUEEN, NOT DARK BUT BEAUTIFUL AND TERRIBLE AS THE DAWN! TEMPESTUOUS AS THE SEA, AND *STRONGER* THAN THE FOUNDATIONS OF THE EARTH! ALL SHALL LOVE ME AND DESPAIR!

Naomi Alderman's novel imagines that if women had *The Power,* men would simply be treated in many of the ways women currently are: at greater risk of sexual violence and with their labour valued less.

IN MY INHERITANCE TRILOGY I CHALLENGE *STEREOTYPICAL* FANTASY WHICH USUALLY PRESENTS A VIRTUOUS STATUS QUO THREATENED BY A DARK OUTSIDER. INSTEAD I PRESENT FLAWED ORDER, AND THE – ALSO FLAWED – EFFORTS TO OVERTHROW IT IN A COMPLEX MULTICULTURAL WORLD.

AUTHOR NK JEMISIN

More complex and intersectional utopic explorations include characters striving *towards* utopia rather than being there. In the Parable series, Octavia Butler critiques cultures which expect women to maintain feminine traits – like empathy – when hypermasculinity is required to survive.

GENDERLESS FUTURE

Other gender utopias imagine different gender systems where there are no genders or multiple genders, or where gender isn't given its current importance.

In *Golden Witchbreed* by Mary Gentle, gender is only chosen at maturity, and has no bearing on social roles, whereas in the *Imperial Radch* trilogy by Ann Leckie, gender is irrelevant.

In *Woman on the Edge of Time* by Marge Piercy, a woman escapes a dystopian present to a future where everyone uses "per" pronouns and lives in harmony, while *The Left Hand of Darkness* by Ursula Le Guin imagines a world where people are both/neither gender. The main characters experience culture shock when trying to impose their understandings of gender and realize how utterly different such a culture is.

IS THE FUTURE INTERSEX, TRANS, OR NON-BINARY?

Sandra Bem (who we met in Chapter 5) initially argued that gender should become an unimportant category, but she changed her view ...

> I PROPOSE THAT WE LET A THOUSAND CATEGORIES OF SEX/GENDER/DESIRE BEGIN TO BLOOM IN ANY AND ALL FLUID AND PERMEABLE CONFIGURATIONS AND, THROUGH THAT VERY PROLIFERATION, THAT WE THEREBY UNDO THE PRIVILEGED STATUS OF THE TWO-AND-ONLY-TWO THAT ARE CURRENTLY TREATED AS NORMAL AND NATURAL.

Bem's idea is that feminism should amplify diverse genders' voices so gender becomes seen as unimportant. This is reflected in some fiction; for example, *Shadow Man* by Melissa Scott, which imagines a future where people have adapted to Ann Fausto-Sterling's idea that there are multiple sex/genders. *2312* by Kim Stanley Robinson poses the question of what would happen if it was discovered that intersex people lived a lot longer than anyone else. Would people shift away from forcing the sex/gender binary on intersex bodies? *Lizard Radio* by Pat Schmatz explores a person growing up non-binary in a rigid gender binary world.

Some of the more recent queer and intersectional authors covered here challenge the dystopia/utopia binary as well as the gender binary, suggesting that non-binary thinking needs to go further than gender.

LIMITS ON IMAGINING THE FUTURE OF GENDER

Authors and readers alike struggle to completely reimagine gender roles and dynamics because they are inevitably shaped by the patriarchal, binary, colonial, capitalist thinking in the world around them.

WHEN I STRIPPED GENDER FROM DESCRIPTIONS OF CHARACTERS IN SPECULATIVE FICTION, PEOPLE COULD STILL TELL THEIR GENDER FROM THE WAY THEY WERE DESCRIBED.

SOCIOLOGIST DANIEL CARDOSO

I HIGHLIGHTED THIS PROBLEM IN MY TWITTER CHALLENGE TO "DESCRIBE YOURSELF AS A MALE AUTHOR WOULD".

WRITER WHITNEY REYNOLDS

Whitney Reynolds ✔
@whitneyarner

new twitter challenge: describe yourself like a male author would

Jennifer Weiner ✔
@jenniferweiner

Her breasts entered the room before her far less interesting face, decidedly maternal hips and rounded thighs. He found her voice unpleasantly audible. As his gaze dropped from her mouth (still talking!) to her cleavage, he wondered why feminists were so angry all the time.

R.A. Williams
@RAWilliams1974

She breasted breastily into the room, not bothering to smile or caring about any aspect of her appearance or its effect on us. She was prepared for the meeting and offered a viable technical solution. We pretended she was invisible, talked over her, and took credit for her idea.

SCI-FI CRITIC & PUBLISHER CHERYL MORGAN

SCI-FI OFTEN ISN'T ABOUT THE FUTURE. THESE IMAGINED FUTURES ARE SIMPLY DISCUSSIONS OF THE PRESENT DRESSED UP WITH SPACESHIPS AND ALIENS AS A MEANS OF ENCOURAGING READERS TO THINK OUTSIDE OF THE BOX.

WHO PRODUCES CULTURE?

As sociologist Ruth Holliday points out, a major issue with popular culture is that those producing it remain overwhelmingly white middle-class men.

The implications of this include the fact that audiences and film students are taught that they can only identify with a white, male protagonist. So, when canonical characters are re-imagined as women and/or people of colour, it often sparks a backlash, as with the all-female *Ghostbusters* – and particularly Leslie Jones. However, *Ghostbusters: Answer The Call* performed well at the box office, and has been followed by similarly popular big-budget women-focused movies such as *Oceans 8* and *Widows*. Despite this popular success, the fourth Ghostbusters movie picks up where the second finished, erasing the story of the all-female third film.

The white male protagonist theory has been soundly disproved by the response to *Star Wars: The Last Jedi* and *Black Panther* – which feature women and non-white actors in key roles. Both fall within the all time top three box office movies at the time of writing. Wakanda forever.

GENDER AS INTERGENERATIONAL TRAUMA

As writer and therapist Alex Iantaffi points out, thinking about the future of gender can alert us to the ways in which gender can be a form of intergenerational trauma, passed on from past, to present, to future generations. Cultural, social, and family-specific gender systems are passed down through the generations, perpetuated because it is too threatening to face up to the harm caused by the ways in which we – and our parents – have done gender.

Stephen King's *It* features an ancient evil which emerges every 27 years in the town of Derry. Despite children going missing, the adults "forget" the bogeyman who haunted their own childhoods and fail to protect their kids from It and from their own neglect and abuse. Gender rules are clearly part of this intergenerational trauma: adults frequently punish boys for being weak, for showing feelings, or for perceived femininity. The one girl in the group is attacked for being both too slutty and too boyish. It's clear that the roots of this trauma lie in settler colonialism, structural racism, patriarchy, and heteronormativity: each time It awakens, it whips up the human forms of hatred and fear that are most prevalent at the time.

WAVES OF PROGRESS AND BACKLASH

We've seen throughout this book how vital it is to be mindful of history when imagining differently gendered futures. We can see how every wave of feminism has received a backlash – most recently in the forms of postfeminism, men's rights activism, and #WomenAgainstFeminism. The trans tipping point was followed by a moral panic, which echoed the panic in the 1980s around the increased visibility of gay men.

Audre Lorde suggests that we shift our attention away from attempting to halt these backlashes and educate our oppressors, and instead towards caring for ourselves and each other, and continuing to imagine better futures.

BLACK AND THIRD WORLD PEOPLE ARE EXPECTED TO EDUCATE WHITE PEOPLE AS TO OUR HUMANITY. WOMEN ARE EXPECTED TO EDUCATE MEN. LESBIANS AND GAY MEN ARE EXPECTED TO EDUCATE THE HETEROSEXUAL WORLD.

THE OPPRESSORS MAINTAIN THEIR POSITION AND EVADE THEIR RESPONSIBILITY FOR THEIR OWN ACTIONS. THERE IS A CONSTANT DRAIN OF ENERGY WHICH MIGHT BE BETTER USED IN REDEFINING OURSELVES AND DEVISING REALISTIC SCENARIOS FOR ALTERING THE PRESENT AND CONSTRUCTING THE FUTURE.

CHAPTER EIGHT: HOW TO THINK ABOUT GENDER

So we near the end of this book. We've learned a lot about gender but have only really scratched the surface of this vast topic. To cover it all, the book would need to be like the Tardis: much bigger on the inside than it appears from the outside. And, like the Tardis, it would need to be moving swiftly through time. As Laurie Penny notes: "The way we think about gender is changing so fast that you can feel the breeze in your hair." How can we draw on what we know about gender now for whatever comes up next?

In this chapter, we'll explore some of the ideas from the "Gender in the Contemporary World" conference (2018) where Francis Ray White and Kit Heyam asked a room full of gender scholars and activists what they wanted everyone to know about gender. Before we start, you might want to reflect on what you've learned from this book. What is gender to you now?

GENDER IS EXTERNAL AND INTERNAL

We've seen how gender is simultaneously:

- Out in the world, in the form of systems and structures of oppression; and
- Inside us in our own gender experiences, expressions, and identities.

WE DON'T EXIST IN A VACUUM. MY BODY, MY IDEAS, AND MY STORIES ARE THE EXPRESSION OF THE IMPERIALIST, WHITE SUPREMACIST, CAPITALIST PATRIARCHY BECAUSE I LIVE IN A WORLD WHERE THOSE ARE THE BUILDING BLOCKS OF EVERYTHING I'VE EVER KNOWN.

SEX AND RELATIONSHIP COACH DAWN SERRA

THERE'S NO MONSTER SEPARATE FROM MYSELF CALLED OPPRESSION THAT CAN BE SLAIN WITH A HERO'S SWORD OR THAT I CAN POINT TO AND SAY "NOT IT".

OPPRESSION

IT IS INSIDE OF ME. IT IS ME. JUST AS IT IS YOU.

WHAT WE DO WITH THAT AND HOW WE RESPOND TO IT IS WHERE THE REAL STORY EMERGES.

GENDER IS A HUGE PART OF HOW THE WORLD WORKS

In Chapter 1 we saw how the systems of patriarchy – interwoven with capitalism and colonialism – have been passed on as each generation teaches the next which bodies, lives, and forms of knowledge and labour are valued and which are not. How can we notice this and stop contributing to this collective trauma?

Literature scholar Priyamvada Gopal suggests a process of decolonizing education. This means first recognizing that education has been produced by the most privileged and powerful in society and has erased the voices of others. Decolonizing education then involves critically examining why we have valued particular forms of knowledge and histories over others. We can do this by drawing on theories and practices from beyond white, Western culture, and bringing in previously overlooked voices – those of women, people of colour, LGBT people, disabled people, and working-class people. This way, everybody learns about the lives of others.

GENDER IS DIVERSE

While patriarchy has dominated everywhere, gender is also hugely diverse and has been experienced, expressed, and identified in very different ways across time and place. The meaning of gender also varies a great deal according to context. As we progress in learning about gender, we might bear in mind Merry E. Wiesner-Hanks' caveat that: "For anything you might want to claim about gender, there'll always be a counterexample."

The lesson here is that it's vital not to impose our ways of understanding and experiencing gender onto anybody else, and to respect the many and varied forms that gender can take as equally valid.

Hopefully we can aim to learn from experiences of gender diversity rather than endeavouring to repress them.

GENDER CAN BE LIMITING

We've seen how damaging gender norms can be for everybody when held tightly and rigidly. For example, we saw that women's identities are often limited to who they are for others. This can close down their potential to find and follow paths and projects that are meaningful to them, as well as meaning their self-esteem is bound up in other people's approval.

Notions that there is "one true way" to be trans or non-binary also constrain people and create shame if they don't fit these "ideals".

The acceptance of toxic forms of masculinity as normal or superior is particularly troubling due to its widespread global impact, for example in the contemporary US Right and in neo-Nazi movements. Scholar Lucy Nicholas points out that it is also implicated in violence, from the domestic sphere to dehumanizing approaches to warfare. Domination over the planet and a sense of entitlement to natural resources, which put us all at risk, can also be linked to hegemonic masculine values.

GENDER CAN BE PAINFUL

Gender norms can also encourage us to blame the wrong people for our gender-related pain: often more marginalized people, rather than those who uphold the dominant norms. This is sometimes called "punching down".

Whitney Phillips notes a similar phenomenon whereby we focus on trolls – or individual abusers – instead of on how omnipresent their views and behaviours are in our culture.

GENDER IS BIOPSYCHOSOCIAL

In Chapter 2 we saw how our sense of our own gender is developed by a complex, ongoing interaction between our bodies and brains ("bio"), what happens to us and what that means to us ("psycho"), and wider cultural messages and social structures around gender ("social"). The common idea that some gender identities or expressions are more real and authentic than others – due to being "natural" – is therefore highly questionable.

Judith Butler's theory of gender performativity points out that we're all always performing our genders. Genders can feel real or natural because we've repeated them so often and had that performance affirmed by others. Our way of doing gender has become ingrained. This also means it isn't easy to choose to perform our genders otherwise.

GENDER IS FLUID AND NON-BINARY

In Chapter 5 we saw that gender shifts over time, and that it can be more useful to see it as existing across multiple spectrums of different traits rather than as one binary of opposites into which all these traits are awkwardly bundled. Gender changes all the time for all of us on multiple, interconnected levels:

Additionally, where we locate ourselves in relation to masculinity and femininity shifts over time, depending on the changing cultural meanings of masculinity and femininity, our own experiences, and how other people read our gender. We might find ourselves in between, both, neither, or beyond this binary altogether.

GENDER IS PERSONAL AND POLITICAL

Because gender is both external and internal, the personal is political and the political is personal. This means that it's important to look through the personal lens and the sociopolitical lens simultaneously, rather than privileging one over the other.

If we see individual people through the sociopolitical lens, we risk objectifying them rather than seeing them as a complex, multifaceted human. If we don't acknowledge the roles of the sociopolitical situation in shaping individual experiences and behaviours – and just focus on each individual person – we risk neglecting to see the very real social systems and cultural norms that impact people's lives.

GENDER IS PLURAL

There is no single story to tell about gender, instead let's embrace its multiplicity of stories.

Sharing our stories of gender connects us and has been vital - from highlighting the omnipresence of sexual violence in women's lives to helping non-binary people make sense of their experiences.

If we can accept the validity of there being multiple stories, then we can stop being so threatened by gender stories that differ from our own. We might also recognize that we can tell multiple possible stories about our own gender experience.

GENDER IS INTERSECTIONAL

Throughout this book we've seen that gender cannot be separated from other intersections like race, class, sexuality, and disability. And that patriarchy is inextricably linked to capitalism, colonialism, white privilege, heteronormativity, ableism, and more. We've seen how these structures of oppression objectify and "other" those whose bodies and labour are deemed less valuable.

It's vital that we recognize the history, impact, and interconnectedness of these systems, and don't prioritize gender over other social categories or experiences.

For example, disability activist, writer, and educator Mia Mingus argues that we all need to recognize our interdependence, rather than accepting a capitalist aim of achieving individual rights for independent women. Journalist Ash Sarkar suggests that we could refocus from the gap between men and women, to those worldwide who are treated as citizen or non-citizen, human or Other.

GENDER IS THEREFORE NOT THE ONLY THING TO FOCUS ON

Those who are marginalized and oppressed by such systems often know the most about them, given that the systems are frequently invisible to those who are privileged by them. Seeing such groups as the experts on these systems would mean that everyone could learn more about how they currently operate, and could operate differently, as well as helpfully shifting the power dynamic from the damaging way it has played out in the past.

We all have unique gender experiences because of the ways in which our gender intersects with our experiences of each of race, class, disability, age, and so on.

GENDER POSITIONS US IN VARIOUS WAYS

It's useful to consider Stephen Karpman's "drama triangle": the idea that - in dynamics between people - we often get drawn into the positions of Persecutor, Rescuer, and Victim.

It's so tempting to assume that we individually can only ever be in the right when it comes to gender - whether as a powerless victim of oppression or a selfless rescuer saving others from abuse and discrimination. However, we all occupy the less "righteous" role of persecutor in different ways: in our complicity within oppressive systems - as apologists and bystanders - as well as in explicitly non-consensual or oppressive acts. We may also sometimes take on the rescuer role in ways which objectify and disempower others - as saviours.

EACH AND EVERY ONE OF US HAS THE CAPACITY TO BE AN OPPRESSOR ... I INVITE US TO INTERROGATE HOW WE MIGHT BE AN OPPRESSOR, AND HOW WE MIGHT BECOME LIBERATORS FOR OURSELVES AND EACH OTHER.

ACTRESS & CAMPAIGNER LAVERNE COX

Audre Lorde encourages us to build self-care into our lives to help us survive where we are oppressed, and confront and address our oppressive tendencies where we're privileged. Without kindness, support, and community, it can be too hard to acknowledge privilege, and too easy to internalize the oppression as shame.

GENDER IS RELEVANT TO EVERYONE

Because gender impacts all of us, it's in all our interests to pay attention to it and to work together towards gender liberation. What might that look like? Well, instead of dividing into "us and them" around gender, we could work together to dismantle rigid, binary, hierarchical systems.

IT IS NOT OUR DIFFERENCES THAT DIVIDE US. IT IS OUR INABILITY TO RECOGNIZE, ACCEPT, AND CELEBRATE THOSE DIFFERENCES.

WE COULD BE MINDFUL OF BOTH THE UNIQUENESS OF OUR GENDER STORIES AND THE WAY THEY CONNECT US WITH OTHERS IN THE PARTS THAT WE SHARE.

WE COULD RECOGNIZE THAT IF OUR PERSONAL LIBERATION COMES WITHOUT THE LIBERATION OF ALL, THEN IT IS MEANINGLESS.

THERE'S OFTEN A HOPE THAT YOUNG PEOPLE WILL CHANGE THINGS. HOWEVER, WE NEED TO BE CAREFUL NOT TO PLACE THE BURDEN ON THE "NEXT GENERATION" AND PASS ON THE INTERGENERATIONAL TRAUMA.

END VIOLENCE AGAINST WOMEN

Everyday Feminism
@EvrydayFeminism
Intersectional feminism for your everyday life!
everydayfeminism.com
113 Following   126.9k Followers

FEAR HAS NO PLACE IN SCHOOL

THOUGHTS & PRAYERS DON'T SAVE LIVES GUN REFORM WILL

*Teen*VOGUE

GENDER IS COMPLICATED, SO KINDNESS IS VITAL

We began this book with Kate Bornstein's ideas on the complexity of gender. Hopefully it has helped you to develop a sense of the ways in which gender is fluid and unstable, as well as giving you some insights into how this complexity came about, and how it operates in our lives.

As we come to a close and find our way towards gender liberation, let's look again to Kate, and to the vital importance of kindness.

FURTHER RESOURCES

These are some of the key resources on gender and related topics that we drew on to write this book.

- Wiesner-Hanks, M. E. (2010). *Gender in History: Global Perspectives.* London: Wiley-Blackwell.
- Connell, R. (2009). *Gender.* Cambridge: Polity.
- Wood, G. W. (2018). *The Psychology of Gender.* London: Routledge.
- Fausto-Sterling, A. (2012). *Sex/Gender: Biology in a Social World.* London: Routledge.
- Fine, C. (2012). *Delusions of Gender.* London: Icon Books.
- Hill-Collins, P. & Bilge, S. (2016). *Intersectionality.* Cambridge: Polity.
- Lorde, A. (2007). *Sister Outsider: Essays and Speeches.* London: Crossing Press.
- Ahmed, S. (2017). *Living a Feminist Life.* Durham, NC: Duke University Press.
- Eddo-Lodge, R. (2017). *Why I'm No Longer Talking to White People About Race.* London: Bloomsbury.
- Gill, R. (2006). *Gender and the Media.* London: Polity Press.
- Lester, CN (2017). *Trans Like Me.* London: Little Brown.
- Richards, C., Bouman, W., & Barker, M-J. (Eds) (2018). *Genderqueer and Non-Binary Genders.* Basingstoke: Palgrave Macmillan.
- Serano, J. (2013). *Excluded: Making Feminist and Queer Movements More Inclusive.* New York, NY: Seal Press.
- Penny, L. (2017). *Bitch Doctrine.* London: Bloomsbury.
- Berila, B. (2016). *Integrating Mindfulness into Anti-Oppression Pedagogy.* London: Routledge.
- Phipps, A. (2018). "Feminism 101". Available from: https://genderate.wordpress.com/feminism-101/

If you want to read the writings of gender theorists and activists (old and new), we've tried to mention as many as possible throughout the book so you can search them out.

The following books are great if you want to think more about gender in your everyday life.

- Iantaffi, A. & Barker, M-J. (2017). *How to Understand Your Gender: A Practical Guide for Exploring Who You Are.* London: Jessica Kingsley.
- Bornstein, K. (2013). *My New Gender Workbook: A Step-by-Step Guide to Achieving World Peace Through Gender Anarchy and Sex Positivity.* London: Routledge.

Also, check out the free zines, podcasts, and posts about gender on Meg-John's websites:

- *rewriting-the-rules.com* and
- *megjohnandjustin.com*

Finally, there are several Icon books on related issues which expand upon material covered in this book. Check out our Graphic Guides to *Queer, Feminism, Critical Theory,* and *Cultural Studies.*

INDEX

ACKNOWLEDGEMENTS AND BIOGRAPHIES

Acknowledgements

Meg-John would like to thank Kiera Jamison, Jules Scheele, Alex Iantaffi, Justin Hancock, Eleanor Janega, Daniel Cardoso and H Howitt for all their help and support during the writing of this book, and all the amazing UK trans and non-binary activists and writers for their inspiration.

Jules would like to thank Meg-John Barker and Kiera Jamison for their patience and support, Mal McKinnon for the pep talks and the offers of company and food, and especially Adrian May: for travelling across the country and taking care of me during illness so I could keep on working, for the constant encouragement and support, and most of all for his faith in me.

Biographies

Meg-John Barker is the author of many popular books on sex, gender, and relationships, including *Queer: A Graphic History* (with Jules Scheele), *How To Understand Your Gender* and *Life Isn't Binary* (with Alex Iantaffi), *Enjoy Sex (How, When, and IF You Want To)* (with Justin Hancock), *Rewriting the Rules*, and *The Psychology of Sex*. They've also written numerous books, articles, chapters, and reports for scholars and counsellors, drawing on their own research and therapeutic practice in these areas. They blog and podcast about these topics on rewriting-the-rules.com and megjohnandjustin.com and they're available for talks, workshops, and writing mentorship. Twitter: @megjohnbarker.

Jules Scheele is a freelance illustrator, comics artist and graphic facilitator based in Glasgow. They specialise in graphic storytelling and illustrations that help translate and bring a human touch to difficult concepts, and their art focuses strongly on mental health, queerness, acitivism and community. From 2014-2018 they ran *One Beat Zines* (onebeatzines.com), a feminist zine collective and distro, with Sarah Broadhurst. Currently they co-run *Ghost Comics Festival* (with João Sobral), a yearly Glasgow-based festival that showcases and celebrates the work of alternative comics artists (ghostcomicsfestival.com). Instagram: @julesscheeleillustration

You can find out about Icon's Introducing Graphic Guide series at introducingbooks.com, including our books in the same size and style as *Gender*: *American Politics*; *Capitalism*; *Feminism*; *Marxism*; and *Queer*.